STEP-BY-STEP

100 Things for Kids to Make and Do

STEP-BY-STEP

100 Things for Kids to Make and Do

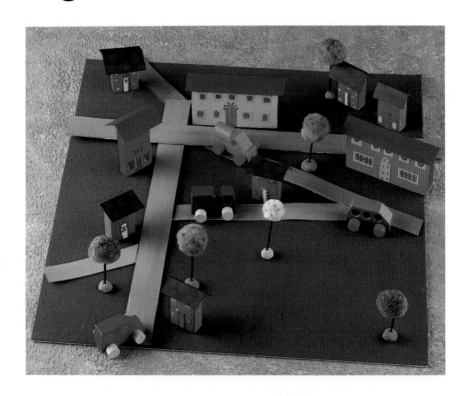

Petra Boase   Marion Elliot   Cecilia Fitzsimons   Judy Williams

Face Painting by Bettina Graham

Photography by James Duncan, John Freeman and Anthony Pickhaver

ANNESS
PUBLISHING

First published in 1996 by Ultimate Editions

© 1996 Anness Publishing Limited

Ultimate Editions is an imprint of
Anness Publishing Limited
1 Boundary Row
London SE1 8HP

ISBN 1 86035 131 X

Publisher: Joanna Lorenz
Series Editor: Lindsay Porter
Assistant Editor: Sarah Ainley
Designers: Peter Laws, Lilian Lindblom
Jacket Design: Caroline Reeves
Photography: John Freeman, James Duncan, Anthony Pickhaver

Typeset by MC Typeset Ltd, Rochester, Kent

Printed and bound in Hong Kong

NOTE

Many of the projects in this book
are very easy and you will be able
to do them by yourself. On some
pages you will see this symbol:

!

This means that the activity may
be dangerous and you must ask
an adult to help you.

CONTENTS

INTRODUCTION

You've read all your books and played with all your toys, so what can you do now?
How about making some of the exciting projects shown in this book!

Before getting to work on the projects, make sure you read the section on
'Getting Started'. This will tell you how to have fun without making too much of
a mess or having an accident. Some of the projects you can make by yourself,
while others will need the help of an adult, but you're sure to want to try them all.

One of the best parts of making the projects is collecting the materials from
around the home. You will be amazed at what you can find! It's a good idea to
keep a box for collecting toilet rolls, cereal boxes, egg cartons, newspaper and
plastic bottles. In a short time, you will have collected all sorts of goodies.
To keep down the cost of the dressing-up projects, try looking in second-hand
shops and flea markets for old clothes and fabrics to cut up and alter according to
the costume. Fabric paints are great for designing your own patterns on the
costumes, but be sure to read the instructions before you begin.
Why not experiment with face paints to complete your disguise?

If you find that you do not have all the materials that you need for a project,
make use of those you already have. If you only have a few colours of paint,
mix them up and create your own colours. Or pick a Nature project instead,
and discover the wonderful world outdoors!

So, whether you're feeling hungry, playful or artistic, there's plenty here
for you to do. Just use your imagination and have some fun!

Getting Started

All the projects in this book can be made easily at home, although some may need adult help. Before you start, read the instructions below to make sure you don't make too much of a mess, and don't have an accident. Remember to ask permission before starting a project and collecting all your materials – you don't want to 'recycle' items which are actually new!

Right: *To prevent your clothes from getting covered in paint and glue, wear a smock or apron, or ask an adult for an old shirt. That way, you can make as much mess as you like!*

Left: *When you have decided which projects you are going to make, lay out all the materials you will need on your work surface. You will then find it much easier to get to work.*

Below: *Before you start work on any project, cover the surface you will be working on with newspaper or an old piece of material.*

Above: *If you can find a clear surface to work on, you'll find it much easier to make your projects. If you are using a desk or kitchen table, clear everything away before you begin so you have plenty of room.*

Left: *It is very important to keep all art materials away from your mouth. Not only will they taste very unpleasant, but they could also be dangerous.*

TECHNIQUES

Papier-mâché

Papier-mâché is made by shredding paper, usually old newspapers, and combining it with glue. The paper can be used in a number of ways to make a huge variety of objects both useful and just for decoration.

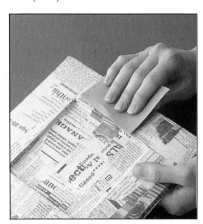

1 For most projects, paper should be torn into fairly short strips approximately 2 cm (¾ in) wide.

2 Mix non-toxic PVA (white) glue with water to the consistency of single (light) cream.

3 Papier-mâché can be pressed into lightly greased moulds or wrapped around cardboard armatures like this.

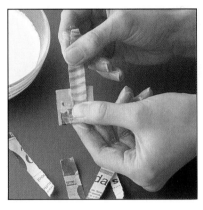

4 To cover smaller shapes, use small, thin pieces of newspaper.

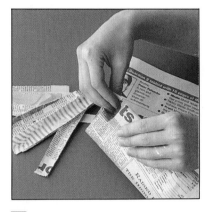

5 Your papier-mâché object may have a slightly rough surface when it has dried out. To make it uniformly smooth, lightly rub the papier-mâché with fine sandpaper.

6 Prime your papier-mâché with two coats of non-toxic white paint to conceal the newsprint surface before decorating.

Salt dough

Salt dough can be used like clay and baked in the oven until hard. Use this recipe for the salt dough projects in the book.

YOU WILL NEED
300 g/11 oz/3 cups plain flour
300 g/11 oz/2 cups, plus 30 ml/2 tbsp salt
wooden spoon
large bowl
30 ml/2 tbsp vegetable oil
200 ml/8 fl oz/1 cup water

1 Put the flour and 300 g/11 oz/2 cups salt into a large bowl.

2 Add the oil to the flour and salt mixture and add the remaining salt. Mix all the ingredients together with a large wooden spoon.

3 Pour in the water and mix thoroughly, making sure there are no lumps.

4 Knead the dough until it is firm.

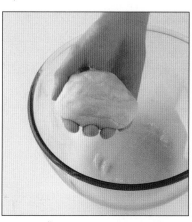

5 When it is ready you can use it straight away or store it in an airtight container in the refrigerator.

Tracing templates

Some of the projects in this book use templates that you can trace. To transfer the template to another piece of paper, follow these simple instructions.

YOU WILL NEED
tracing paper
pencil
card (cardboard) or paper

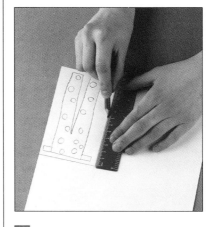

1 Place a piece of tracing paper over the template and draw around the shape using a pencil. The outline should be dark and heavy.

2 Take the tracing paper off the template and turn it over. Rub over the traced image with a pencil on the reverse side of paper.

3 Place the tracing on a piece of card (cardboard) or paper with the rubbed pencil side facing down. Draw over the lines you have made with a pencil to transfer the picture.

Scaling-up

Sometimes you will want to make a project bigger than the template given. It's easy to make it larger. This is known as scaling-up.

1 Draw a box around your original shape. Draw two diagonal lines through the box and to the top edge of the page.

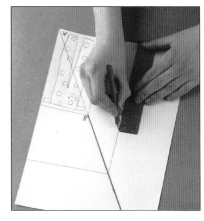

2 Draw a box as large as you want your scaled-up image to be.

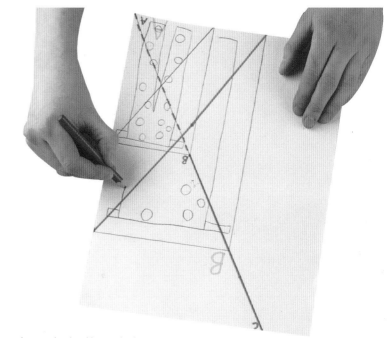

3 Draw the newly-sized image in the box, looking very carefully at the original.

Stencilling

Stencilling is a way of applying decoration to a surface using special card (cardboard), clear film or metal stencils. A shape is drawn onto the card, cut out, and then paint is applied over the cut-out portion of the stencil with a sponge or brush. It is possible to buy ready-cut stencils or you can make your own. Ask an adult to cut out your stencil motif for you – craft knives are *very* sharp, and are difficult to control.

1 Cut a piece of stencil card (cardboard) and draw your design.

2 Ask an adult to cut out the image from the stencil card.

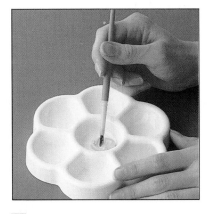

3 Mix paint in a palette or on an old saucer. Add a little water to make a slightly sticky consistency.

4 Cut a piece of household sponge into small squares.

5 Place the stencil card on a piece of heavy paper or thin card (posterboard). Dip the sponge in paint and gently dab it over the cut-out motif.

6 Remove the stencil card carefully, one corner at a time, to avoid smudging the paint.

Bird Mosaic Tray

This tray will make the simplest meal look exciting! Mosaic has been used as a decorative device for centuries, and especially fine examples were made by the Romans to decorate the floors of their villas. The look of mosaic has been imitated here by the use of irregular squares cut from scraps of coloured paper. The tray is sealed with several coats of varnish so it can be wiped clean with a damp cloth after use.

YOU WILL NEED
wooden tray
fine sandpaper
diluted non-toxic PVA (white) glue
paintbrushes
non-toxic white paint
non-toxic bright paint
scissors
thin paper in a variety of colours
pencil
non-toxic clear gloss varnish
   (optional)

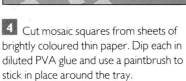

paint

sandpaper

scissors

paintbrushes

paper glue

pencil

paper

1 Rub down the surface of the wooden tray with fine sandpaper. Seal the tray with a coat of diluted PVA (white) glue.

2 Prime the tray with a coat of white paint and allow to dry.

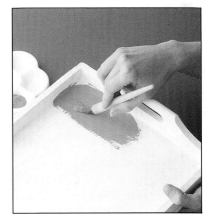

3 Paint the tray with two coats of bright paint and allow to dry thoroughly.

4 Cut mosaic squares from sheets of brightly coloured thin paper. Dip each in diluted PVA glue and use a paintbrush to stick in place around the tray.

5 Draw and cut a bird shape from paper and stick it in place in the centre of the tray. Add details cut from contrasting papers and allow the tray to dry overnight.

6 Seal the tray with several coats of diluted PVA glue or clear gloss varnish.

Rubber-stamped Stationery

If you're looking for unusual stationery, why not cut stamps from small erasers to decorate writing paper and envelopes? You could press them onto different-coloured ink pads or into bright paint to make your own personal stationery. You must ask an adult to cut the eraser for you – craft knives are *very* sharp.

YOU WILL NEED
pencil
rubber erasers
craft knife
non-toxic ink pad
writing paper

ink pad

pencil

erasers

writing paper

1 Draw your design onto the face of the eraser.

2 Ask an adult to trim carefully around the design with a craft knife to leave a raised image.

3 Gently press the eraser onto the ink pad. Test it first on a scrap of paper to make sure that enough ink has been absorbed to make a dark image.

4 Press the eraser firmly onto the writing paper. Remove it carefully to avoid smudging the ink.

Stencilled Snap Cards

A game of snap is always good fun – why not make your own set of cards like this cheerful version? The cards are stencilled with different colours and are bright and simple. Each stencil can be used several times if allowed to dry thoroughly between colours. You must ask an adult to cut out the stencils for you – craft knives are *very* sharp.

YOU WILL NEED
stencil card (cardboard)
ruler
pencil
scissors
craft knife
heavy paper in four different colours
small squares of household sponge
non-toxic paint in four different colours
non-toxic paper glue
medium-weight coloured card (posterboard)

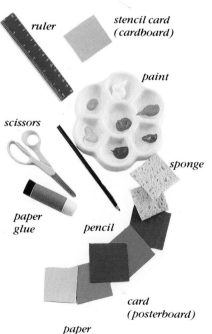

ruler

stencil card (cardboard)

paint

scissors

sponge

paper glue

pencil

card (posterboard)

paper

1 Cut four pieces of stencil card (cardboard) measuring approximately 6 × 9 cm (2¼ × 3½ in).

2 Draw four different symbols on the stencil card. Ask an adult to cut out the shapes for you with a craft knife.

3 Cut rectangles of coloured paper measuring 6.5 × 8.5 cm (2½ × 3¼ in). Place the first stencil on one of the rectangles. With a sponge square, dab paint over the stencil until the cut-out space is covered. Carefully remove the stencil, taking care not to smudge the paint. Repeat with all the stencils until you have made enough cards.

4 Stick each stencilled rectangle onto a slightly larger piece of medium-weight card (posterboard). Allow the glue to dry thoroughly before you play snap.

PLAYING SNAP

To play, deal out all the cards to each player. In turn, discard one card onto a central pile. If two cards of the same pair are played in sequence, the first player to notice must shout 'snap' and grab the pair. The player with the most pairs at the end of the game wins. It sounds simple, but try playing very quickly!

Woven Paper Cards

Paper weaving is a fun way to achieve exciting effects from a very simple process. Pick your papers with care so that the colours complement each other, or contrast in interesting ways. You can use the weaving as a design on its own, or mount it behind shaped frames to make unusual greetings cards.

YOU WILL NEED
medium-weight card (posterboard) in
   a variety of colours
ruler
pencil
scissors
heavy paper in a variety of colours
non-toxic paper glue

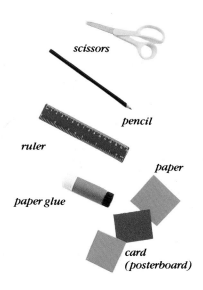

scissors

pencil

ruler

paper

paper glue

card
(posterboard)

1 Draw a rectangle measuring 16 × 24 cm (6¼ × 9½ in) on medium-weight green card (posterboard) and cut it out. Draw a line down the centre of the rectangle and, with adult help, gently score along it with scissors to form a fold.

2 Mark a 9 cm (3½ in) square on the front of the card and cut it out to form a window.

3 Cut a piece of red card measuring 10 × 10 cm (4 × 4 in). Make vertical cuts every 1 cm (⅜ in) down the card, from just below the top edge almost to the bottom, but do not cut all the way through.

4 Cut several strips of orange paper approximately 1 cm (⅜ in) wide.

5 Weave the orange strips through the red to make a checked pattern. Trim and attach the orange strips at each side of the card with paper glue.

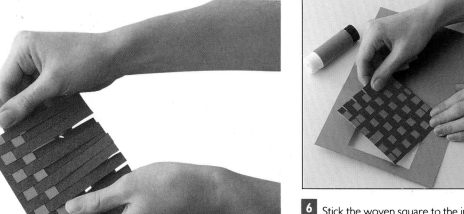

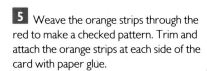

6 Stick the woven square to the inside front of the card so that it shows through the window.

Little Town

Make your own dream town out of small boxes and card (cardboard). Include all your favourite shops, your school and your friends' houses.

YOU WILL NEED

different-sized boxes (matchboxes are
 ideal)
card (cardboard)
scissors
PVA (white) glue
coloured paper
coloured paints
paintbrush
toothpicks
green pom-poms
green glitter
plasticine
green sticky-backed (adhesive) felt

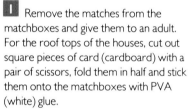

glitter *paper*

plasticine

pom-pom

paintbrush

matchbox

scissors

masking tape

toothpicks

PVA (white) glue

paints

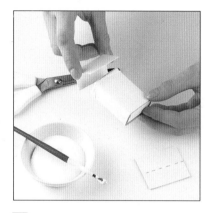

1 Remove the matches from the matchboxes and give them to an adult. For the roof tops of the houses, cut out square pieces of card (cardboard) with a pair of scissors, fold them in half and stick them onto the matchboxes with PVA (white) glue.

2 Cover the houses in different-coloured sheets of paper and paint on doors and windows.

3 For the trees, paint the toothpicks brown. Glue a green pom-pom (see the Clown's Outfit project on page 88 for instructions but substitute fabric with wool) onto a toothpick and cover it in glue. Dab the pom-pom into a ball of green glitter and paint on some red spots. To make the tree stand up, stick it into a piece of plasticine.

4 For the roads, cut out strips of card and paint them.

5 Cover a large piece of card with green sticky-backed (adhesive) felt.

6 Arrange the houses, trees and roads around the green felt to create the town. If you don't glue the pieces down, you can change the position of the buildings as many times as you like and store the town away easily.

Magnetic Fish Game

This is a version of an old and much-loved game that has been played by generations of children. To make the game more competitive, you could write a score on the back of each fish. The player with the highest score wins.

YOU WILL NEED
scraps of heavy coloured paper
pencil
scissors
wax crayons
paper clips
thin wooden sticks
thin coloured cord
small horseshoe magnet

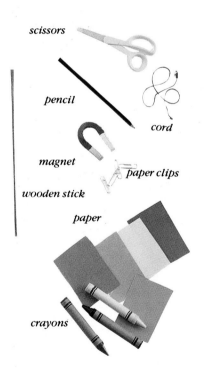

scissors

pencil

cord

magnet

paper clips

wooden stick

paper

crayons

1 Draw fish shapes onto the scraps of paper and cut them out.

2 Decorate the fish using wax crayons.

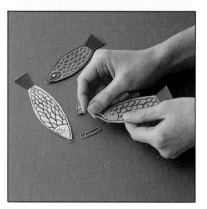

3 Attach a paper clip to the nose of each fish so that it can be picked up by the fishing line.

4 To make the fishing rod, tie a length of cord to the wooden dowel and tie a small magnet to the end of the line.

Paper Doll

You can make all kinds of outfits for this little doll.
Make some friends and family for her to play with,
or even some pets.

YOU WILL NEED
tracing and plain paper for template
pencil
card (cardboard)
scissors
white paper
coloured paints
paintbrush
shoe box

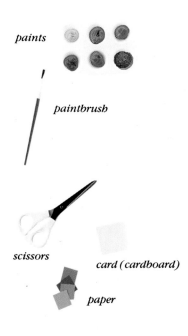

paints

paintbrush

scissors

card (cardboard)

paper

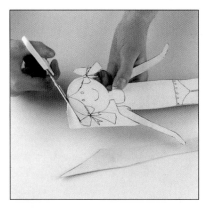

1 For the doll, scale-up the template from the back of the book following the instructions on page 12. Trace her onto a piece of card (cardboard). Cut out the doll carefully with a pair of scissors.

2 Paint the doll's face, hair, and underwear. Leave to dry.

3 Trace around the doll to make the clothes and paint them in bright colours. When you cut out the clothes make sure you leave small tags on them. These will bend behind the doll to stop them from falling off.

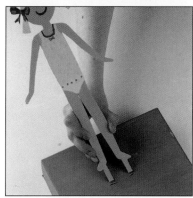

4 Paint the lid of a shoe box and make two holes with a pair of scissors to support the doll. Dress up the doll in her various outfits, remembering to bend the tags behind her.

Dressing-up Doll

Shiver me timbers! Here's a brawny brigand for you to
dress! Why not make a parrot to sit on his shoulder
and keep him company on the high seas?

YOU WILL NEED
tracing paper or graph paper
pencil
thin white card (posterboard)
cartridge (construction) paper
scissors
paintbrushes
non-toxic paint in a variety of colours

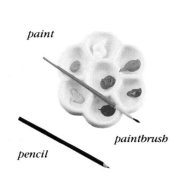

paint

paintbrush

pencil

scissors

*card
(posterboard)*

tracing paper

*cartridge
(construction) paper*

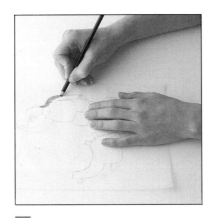

1 Trace or scale up the pirate and his
clothes from the template at the back
of the book.

2 Transfer the pirate to thin card
(posterboard), and the clothes to
cartridge (construction) paper. Carefully
cut them out.

3 Fill in the pirate's features with paint.
Paint his underclothes in bright colours
and decorate the pirate's clothes.

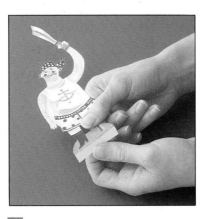

4 With adult help, lightly score and fold
the base of the pirate so that he stands up.

5 Bend the tabs of the clothes over.
Place them on the pirate and squeeze the
tabs closed so that they fit snugly over the
paper figure.

Matchbox Theatre

This must be the smallest theatre in the world – you can almost carry it in your pocket.

YOU WILL NEED
kitchen matchbox
scissors
coloured paints
paintbrush
coloured paper
felt-tip pen
coloured sticky-tape

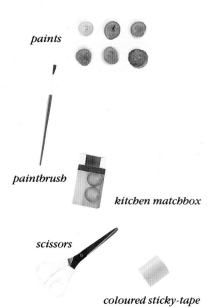

paints

paintbrush

kitchen matchbox

scissors

coloured sticky-tape

paper

1 Remove the matches from the box and give them to an adult. Take the matchbox apart and cut one-third off the sleeve with a pair of scissors. Paint both the sleeve and tray and leave them to dry before putting them back together.

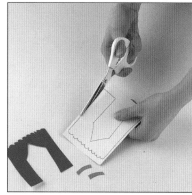

2 Draw the curtains on a piece of coloured paper with a felt-tip pen and cut them out.

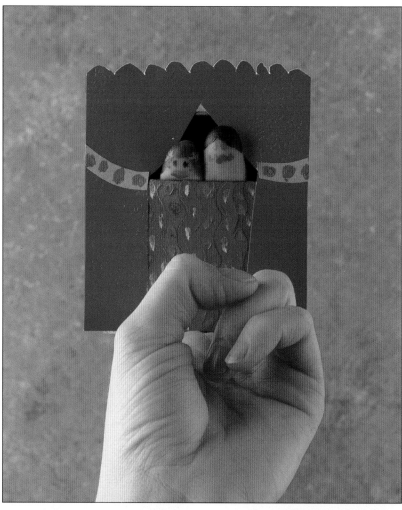

3 Attach the curtains to the matchbox using coloured sticky-tape.

4 Paint a face onto the palm side of your middle and index fingers and put them inside the theatre to start acting.

26

Jigsaw Puzzle

Challenge your family and friends with this home-made jigsaw puzzle.

YOU WILL NEED
colourful picture or large photograph
   of your choice
card (cardboard)
PVA (white) glue
scissors
pencil
paintbrush

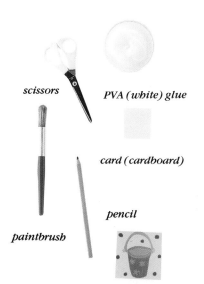

scissors

PVA (white) glue

card (cardboard)

pencil

paintbrush

picture

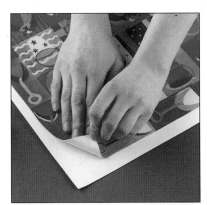

1 Stick your picture onto a piece of card (cardboard) with PVA (white) glue. Rub the palm of your hand over the picture to make sure it is completely smooth. Allow it to dry.

2 Cut around the picture with a pair of scissors to remove the excess card.

CRAFT HINT
You could cut out a picture from a magazine rather than using a photograph.

3 Draw the jigsaw pieces onto the reverse of the picture with a pencil.

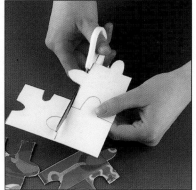

4 Carefully cut out the jigsaw shapes and keep them in a safe place.

Eye Masks

Even if you're not going to a masked ball, you'll have fun making and wearing these disguises! They're especially good if you're in a play or pantomime – you'll be surprised how difficult your friends find it to recognize you!

YOU WILL NEED
tracing paper or graph paper
pencil
thin card (posterboard) in a variety of colours
scissors
paper in a variety of colours
non-toxic paper glue
thin wooden sticks
paintbrush
non-toxic paint
non-toxic strong glue
wax crayons
gold paper

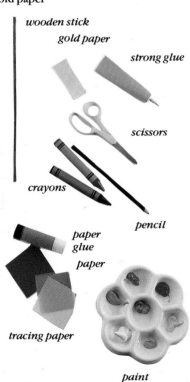

wooden stick
gold paper
strong glue
scissors
crayons
pencil
paper glue
paper
tracing paper
paint

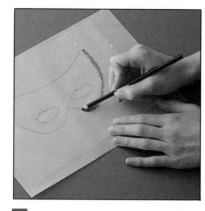

1 Trace or scale up the fiery mask shape from the template at the back of the book and transfer to orange card (posterboard). Cut it out.

2 Place the card on purple paper. Extend the sides and top of the eye mask with small spikes. Cut out this shape.

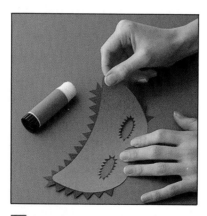

3 Using paper glue stick the orange shape in place on top of the purple one. Carefully trim the lower edge of the mask if necessary.

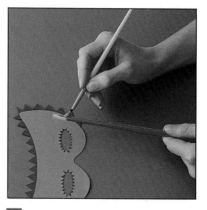

4 Paint the wooden stick a bright colour. You may have to use two coats of paint.

5 Attach the wooden stick to the side of the mask with strong glue. Stick it the right of the mask if you are right-handed and vice-versa if you are left-handed.

6 To make the leopard mask, use yellow card and apply the spots with wax crayon. The king has a crown made of gold paper, and his eyebrows are applied with wax crayon.

Paper Plate Tennis

A fun game for two or more players to play around the house or outdoors.

YOU WILL NEED
4 paper plates
coloured paints
paintbrush
scissors
coloured sticky-tape
ping-pong ball

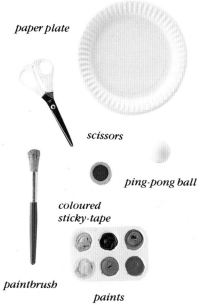

paper plate

scissors

ping-pong ball

coloured sticky-tape

paintbrush

paints

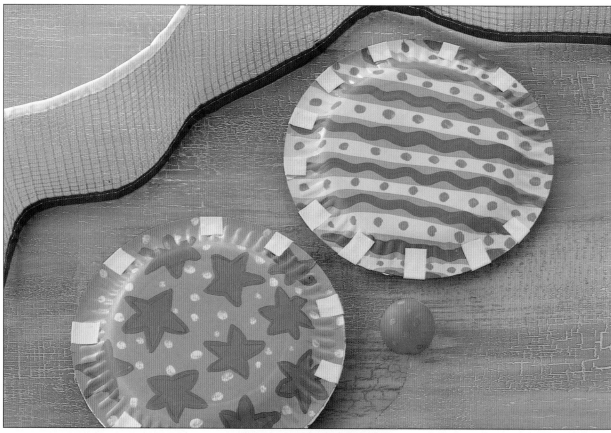

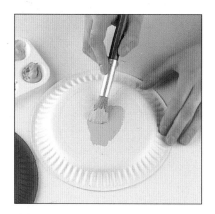

1 For each 'racquet' you will need two paper plates. Paint each plate a plain colour. Allow to dry.

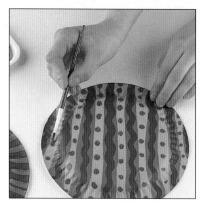

2 Paint patterns onto the plates and leave to dry.

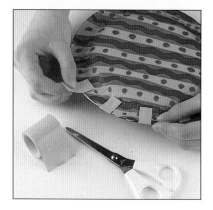

3 Attach the plates with pieces of coloured sticky-tape, leaving a gap big enough for your hand to slide in.

4 Paint the ping-pong ball. Now you are ready to start playing.

Origami Water Bomb

Seek revenge outdoors with this crafty piece of paper
work, but be sure to clear up afterwards!

YOU WILL NEED
pencil
ruler
coloured paper
scissors
water

scissors

paper

1 Measure a piece of paper 20 cm ×
20 cm (8 in × 8 in). Cut it out with a pair
of scissors. Draw lines across the square
following the template at the back of
the book and fold along them to make
creases. Take the two creases either side
of the square and pinch them into the
centre. Press flat to form a triangle.

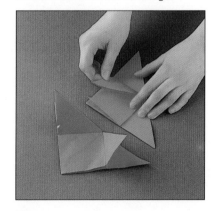

2 Fold back the corners of the triangle
on both sides to form a square shape.

3 Turn the side corners of the square
into the centre. Turn it over and do the
same again. Turn the top points into the
slots. Turn it over and do the same again.

4 At one end of the bomb there is a
small hole. Blow into it hard to make a
cube. Through the hole, fill the bomb with
water and you are ready to have some
outdoor fun!

Paper Beads

These fun and colourful beads are made from the pages of a magazine, but no one will guess when you wear them.

YOU WILL NEED
tracing and plain paper for templates
felt-tip pen
scissors
colourful pictures from magazines
PVA (white) glue
wooden stick or knitting needle
embroidery thread

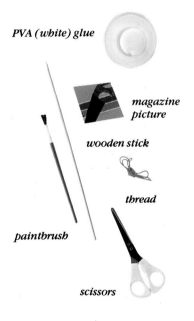

PVA (white) glue

magazine picture

wooden stick

thread

paintbrush

scissors

1 Trace the templates from the back of the book following the instructions on page 12. Place the templates onto the colourful magazine pictures and draw around them.

2 Cut out the shapes with scissors.

3 Paint a line of PVA (white) glue in the middle of the shapes and wrap them tightly around a wooden stick or a knitting needle. Carefully remove the stick or knitting needle.

4 When the glue has dried, thread the beads onto a piece of embroidery thread to make either a necklace or a bracelet and tie a knot.

Cowboy Face Mask

Ride the range in this cowboy mask! Wear a bright scarf around your neck for added authenticity and you'll be the envy of every cowpoke in town!

YOU WILL NEED
heavy light blue, dark blue and orange paper
pencil
scissors ruler
non-toxic paper glue
sticky tape
stapler

scissors

stapler

sticky tape

pencil

paper glue

paper

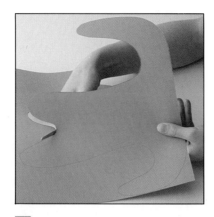

1 Draw a hat on the light blue paper. Draw a thin band approximately 5 × 60 cm (2 × 24 in) on the same paper. Cut them out.

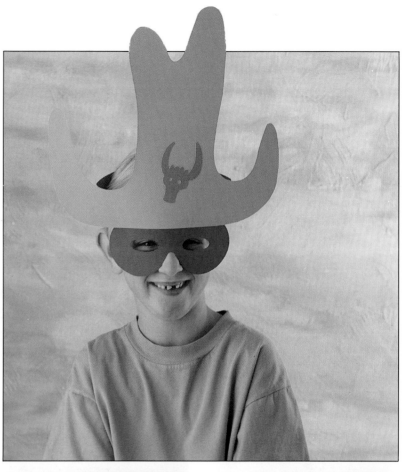

2 Draw a steer's head on the orange paper and cut it out. Stick it to the front of the hat with paper glue.

3 Draw and cut out the eye mask from the dark blue paper. Stick it to the back of the hat with sticky tape.

4 Stick the hat band to the back of the hat with paper glue. Make sure that it is not visible from the front. To give additional strength, hold the band in place with a strip of sticky tape. Hold the hat band around the head and ask a friend to mark where the two ends overlap. Remove the hat and with adult help, staple or glue the ends neatly together.

Papier-mâché Necklace

Papier-mâché is made by recycling old paper and cardboard; why not carry on this ecological theme by decorating a papier-mâché necklace with daisies and insects – you'll blend in well at any garden party!

YOU WILL NEED
large coin, for tracing circles
corrugated cardboard
pencil
scissors
newspaper
diluted non-toxic PVA (white) glue
non-toxic white paint
paintbrush
non-toxic paint in a variety of colours
non-toxic clear gloss varnish
darning needle
non-toxic strong glue
eye pins
coloured cord

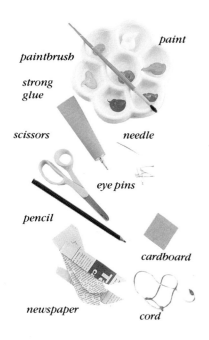

paint

paintbrush

strong
glue

scissors

needle

eye pins

pencil

cardboard

newspaper

cord

1 Place a round object such as a coin on the cardboard. Draw around it to make 12 discs and cut them out.

2 Cover each disc with three layers of thin papier-mâché strips. Leave them to dry overnight.

3 Prime each disc with two coats of white paint and leave to dry.

4 Draw a daisy or ladybird (ladybug) on each disc. Fill in the design with paints.

5 Seal each disc with two coats of gloss varnish. When they are dry, with adult help, make a hole in the top of each with a darning needle. Dab a little strong glue over each hole and push in an eye pin.

6 Cut a length of cord. Pass the cord through the eye pin of each disc and tie it before adding the next.

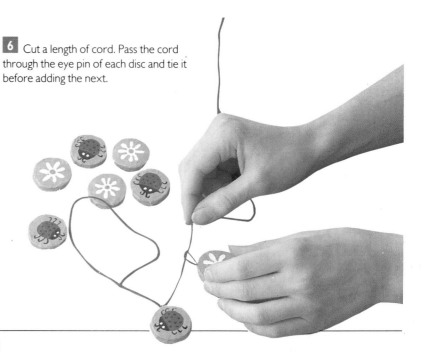

Painted Postcards

Be original and make your own cards. This ingenious method of applying and scratching off paint gives very professional looking results, and the cards could be used for place names and invitations to special events as well as birthdays and Christmas.

YOU WILL NEED
heavy coloured paper
ruler
pencil
scissors
gold paper
paintbrush
non-toxic paint in a variety of colours
non-toxic paper glue

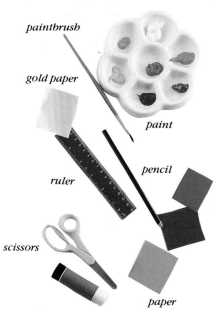

paintbrush

gold paper

paint

ruler

pencil

scissors

paper

paper glue

1 Measure and cut out rectangles of coloured paper measuring 10 × 12 cm (4 × 4¾ in).

2 Cut smaller rectangles of gold paper.

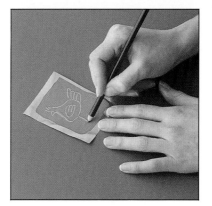

3 Apply a coat of paint to the gold paper, and while it is still wet draw a simple design in the paint with a soft pencil. Allow the paint to dry thoroughly.

4 Cut around the scratched images leaving a small border. Stick each one to a rectangle of coloured paper with paper glue and allow to dry.

Printed Wrapping Paper

If you don't like the gift wrap you see in stationery shops, print your own using stamps cut from foam rubber. It is very satisfying to be congratulated on wrapping paper *and* gift!

YOU WILL NEED
heavy corrugated cardboard
pencil
ruler
scissors
non-toxic strong glue
foam rubber approximately 6 mm
　(¼ in) thick
non-toxic paint in a variety of colours
thin coloured paper

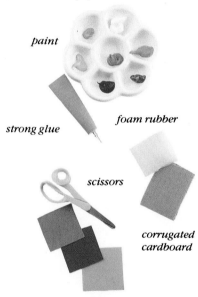

paint

strong glue

foam rubber

scissors

corrugated cardboard

paper

1 To make the stamps, cut several rectangles of heavy cardboard measuring 5 × 6 cm (2 × 2¼ in). Cut an equal number of smaller rectangles measuring 6 × 1.5 cm (2¼ × ⅝ in) to form the handles. Stick the handles to the top of the bases and leave to dry.

2 Draw the image for each stamp onto the piece of foam rubber. Carefully cut around each shape with scissors ensuring that the edges are smooth.

3 Stick the shapes to the base of each stamp and allow to dry thoroughly.

4 Spread a thin layer of paint onto a saucer to act as an ink pad. Press each stamp into the paint, varying the colours as desired, and print the wrapping paper.

Fancy Wrapped Parcels

Turn the humblest present into an exciting parcel by making the wrappings interesting and fun. All sorts of characters are appropriate for decorating parcels. Think of the person who will receive the parcel, and of their favourite characters when choosing a design.

YOU WILL NEED
items to wrap
crêpe paper
sticky tape
paper ribbon
pencil
thin paper in a variety of colours
scissors
non-toxic paper glue
non-toxic strong glue

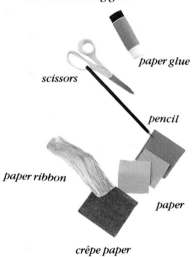

paper glue

scissors

pencil

paper ribbon

paper

crêpe paper

1 Wrap the parcels in crêpe paper.

2 Open out lengths of paper ribbon and secure each parcel.

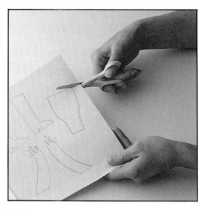

3 Draw designs onto pieces of thin coloured paper to make the head, arms and legs for each parcel (or head, legs and tail if an animal). Cut out the shapes.

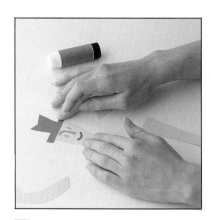

4 Stick the decorative details onto each main body piece with paper glue.

5 Stick the decorations around the corners of each parcel with strong glue.

Christmas Wreath

Celebrate the festive season with this Christmas wreath. The leaves are lightly scored so that they have a three-dimensional effect. Use gold paper to impart an extra sparkle to the musical angel.

YOU WILL NEED
heavy red paper
ruler
pencil
scissors
tracing paper
green, white, gold and pink paper
small stapler
non-toxic paper glue
paper ribbon
thin cord

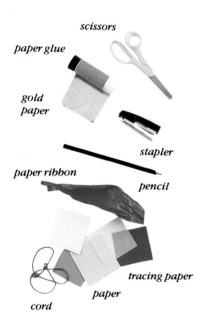

scissors
paper glue
gold paper
stapler
paper ribbon
pencil
paper
tracing paper
cord

1 Draw a circle measuring 24 cm (9½ in) in diameter on a square of heavy red paper. Cut it out.

2 Trace the leaf shape from the template and transfer it to the green paper. Cut out approximately 30 leaves.

3 To make the leaves appear three-dimensional, ask an adult to help you score the centre of each one with a pair of scissors and curve the paper. Score half the leaves on the front and half on the back, so that they curve around the right- and left-hand sides of the wreath.

4 With adult help, staple the leaves around both sides of the wreath, overlapping them slightly.

5 Trace the angel pieces from the template and transfer them to white, gold and pink paper. Cut out each of the pieces, and stick them in place on the front of the wreath.

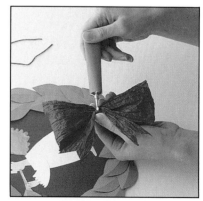

6 Open out a length of paper ribbon and tie it to form a bow. Stick it in position at the bottom of the wreath. Stick a loop of cord to the back to form a hanger.

CRAFT FUN

Potato Printing

Create your own wrapping paper with this simple and fun technique.

YOU WILL NEED
potato
knife
felt-tip pen
coloured ink
paper towel
paper plate or saucer for the ink
white or coloured paper

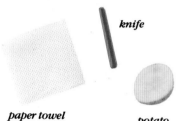

paper

ink

paper towel

knife

potato

paper plate

felt-tip pen

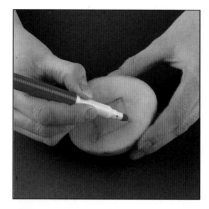

1 Cut a potato in half with a sharp knife and draw out a shape with a felt-tip pen.

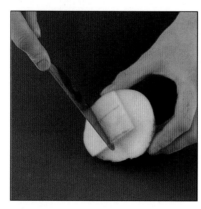

2 With the help of an adult, cut out the area around the shape.

3 Pour a few drops of ink onto a piece of paper towel placed on a paper plate or saucer and dab the potato into it.

4 Place the potato onto some white or coloured paper and press down hard. Repeat this process until the paper is covered with the design.

String Printing

Print this string design on coloured paper and cover your school textbooks.

YOU WILL NEED
cardboard
scissors
PVA (white) glue
felt-tip pen
string
saucer or paper plate
coloured paints
paintbrush
coloured paper

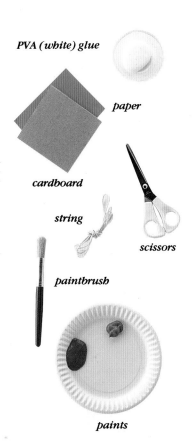

PVA (white) glue

paper

cardboard

string

scissors

paintbrush

paints

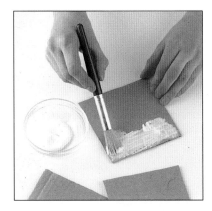

1 Cut out a few pieces of cardboard with a pair of scissors and stick the pieces together with PVA (white) glue to make a thick block.

2 Draw a design onto the cardboard with the felt-tip pen.

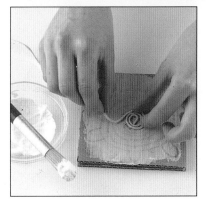

3 Cover the cardboard with glue and stick the string around the outline of the design. Allow to dry.

4 Dab paint onto the block with a paintbrush. Press down onto the paper. Repeat this process until the paper is covered with the design.

Teasel Mice

In days gone by, teasels were used to comb or 'tease' tangled wool before it could be spun. You can use them to make a family of animals.

YOU WILL NEED
teasels
scissors
circle of material 23 cm (9 in) in
  diameter for the body
needle, thread and pins
soft toy stuffing
rectangle of material 23 cm × 10 cm
  (9 in × 4 in) for the arms
rectangle of material 40 cm × 10 cm
  (15 in × 4 in) for the skirt
PVA (white) glue
beads for nose and eyes
fishing line or thread for whiskers
bits and pieces of felt, string, lace
  and ribbon

teasel

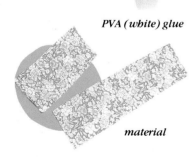

soft toy stuffing

PVA (white) glue

material

lace

scissors

! **1** Collect teasels from hedges and roadsides. Cut the heads from the stalks. Be careful, they are extremely prickly. If you have trouble finding any, teasels are often sold in florists' shops for dried flower arrangements. Alternatively, you can make these mice with pine cones instead.

! **2** Sew a running stitch around the edge of the circle of cloth for the body. Pull the threads to gather.

3 Put some of the toy stuffing in the middle.

4 Put a teasel on top of the stuffing. Draw the gathering thread in tightly around the base of the teasel. Knot to secure.

5 To make the arms, fold the small rectangle of material in half. Fold in half again. Pin and stitch along its length.

6 Sew a running stitch along one long side of the large rectangle of material for the skirt. Gather. Place around the neck of the teasel and stitch so that the skirt hangs over the body. Put the arms around the neck and stitch them in place above the skirt. Finish by gluing on beads for the eyes and nose, whiskers of fishing line or thread, felt ears and string for the tail. Decorate with ribbon, lace, hats, aprons, cloaks and other clothes. Make a whole family of mice!

Papier-mâché Piggy Bank

You won't find a friendlier pig to look after your pocket money!

YOU WILL NEED
PVA (white) glue
water
vaseline (optional)
large bowl
newspaper
wooden stick
balloon
pin
egg carton
scissors
masking tape
coloured paints
paintbrush

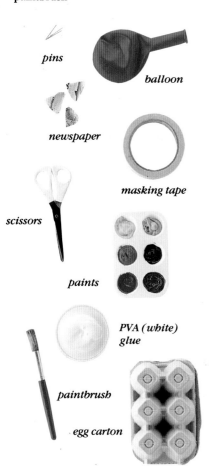

pins

balloon

newspaper

masking tape

scissors

paints

PVA (white) glue

paintbrush

egg carton

1 For the papier-mâché, mix some PVA (white) glue with water in a large bowl and stir in several layers of torn-up newspaper with a wooden stick. Blow up the balloon and tie a knot in it. Cover the balloon with water or vaseline and apply a layer of newspaper, then apply five layers of papier-mâché. Leave the balloon to dry overnight in a warm place. (This may take a little longer depending on the time of year.)

2 Once the papier-mâché is completely dry, burst the balloon with a pin and remove it. You may need to make a small hole to take out the balloon. For the feet and snout, cut up an egg carton with a pair of scissors, dividing up the egg tray and attaching the parts onto the balloon with masking tape.

3 Cut out triangles from the egg carton for the ears and attach them to the balloon with masking tape. Use papier-mâché to cover over the feet, snout and ears.

4 For the tail, roll up a piece of newspaper tightly and apply glue to secure it. Wrap the strip around your finger and let go. It should now have a coil shape. Attach it to the balloon with strips of papier-mâché.

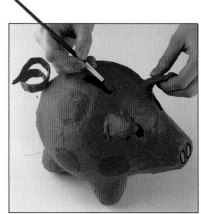

5 When all the papier-mâché is completely dry, apply two coats of paint to the pig.

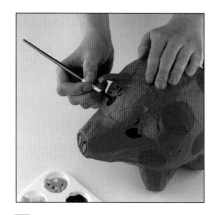

6 Cut out the money slot and finish painting the details onto the pig.

Decoupage Frame

Decoupage is a form of decoration using pictures cut from magazines, newspapers, even wallpaper. The pictures are then stuck onto mirror frames, screens and all sorts of objects to make a new and interesting design. Black and white pictures can be hand-tinted with paint that matches or contrasts with the object you are decorating. You can dip the pictures in cold tea to give the paper a pleasing 'aged' effect similar to old photos, or you can colour them with paints.

YOU WILL NEED
painted picture frame
sandpaper
assorted black and white pictures
scissors
non-toxic paint that matches the
    colour of the frame
undiluted non-toxic PVA (white) glue
paintbrush
non-toxic clear gloss varnish

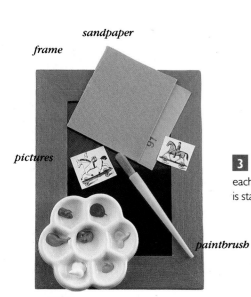

sandpaper
frame
pictures
paintbrush
paint

1 Remove the glass and backing from the picture frame. Lightly rub down the paint with sandpaper to give a patchy, antiqued effect.

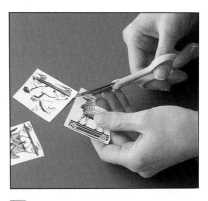

2 Carefully trim the pictures, leaving a slight border around the edges.

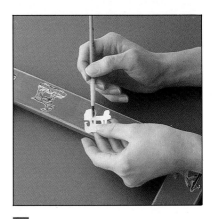

4 Arrange the dried cut-outs around the frame. When you are pleased with the composition, stick them in place with PVA (white) glue.

3 Make a thin solution of paint and dip each cut-out briefly into it until the paper is stained. Leave the cuttings flat to dry.

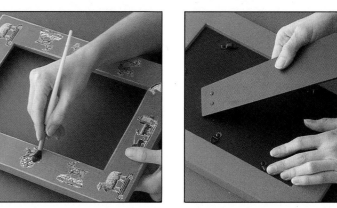

5 Seal the frame with three or four coats of gloss varnish. Leave to dry.

6 Fit your picture inside and replace the glass and backing.

Juggling Squares

Keep practising your juggling skills and impress everyone around you.

YOU WILL NEED
squares of colourful fabric
pencil
ruler
scissors
pins
needle
thread
crumpled paper or newspaper

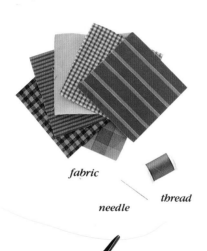

fabric

thread

needle

scissors

crumpled paper

pins

IMPORTANT SAFETY NOTE

You may need an adult's help for the sewing.

1 For each juggling square you will need six squares of fabric, 12 cm × 12 cm (4¾ in × 4¾ in). Cut these out with a pair of scissors. With the right sides facing each other sew the first two squares together with a needle and thread, allowing a 1 cm (½ in) seam allowance.

2 Sew all the squares together to form a letter 'T' shape.

3 Join the sides together to form a cube, leaving one side open for the stuffing. Turn the cube right side out.

4 Fill the cube with the crumpled paper or newspaper, and, when it is full, sew up the last side.

Teddy Bear's Outfit

Spoil your teddy with a new set of clothes.

YOU WILL NEED
scissors
colourful felt
needle
cotton thread
ribbon
PVA (white) glue
paintbrush
tracing and plain paper for templates
pencil
buttons
ruler
cotton fringing

thread

needle

PVA (white) glue

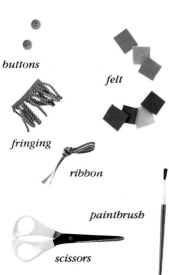

buttons

felt

fringing

ribbon

paintbrush

scissors

1 With a pair of scissors, cut out two semi-circular pieces of colourful felt to fit the width of your teddy's head. Sew the two pieces together with a needle and thread. To decorate the hat, stick on some felt shapes and ribbon with PVA (white) glue.

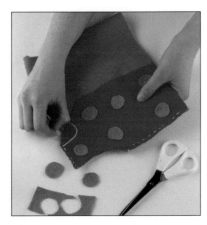

2 For the waistcoat, scale-up and trace the templates from the back of the book following the instructions on page 12. Place the templates onto pieces of felt and cut out. Glue on some felt spots and sew the three pieces together.

3 Sew three buttons onto one side of the waistcoat.

4 For the scarf, cut out a 30 cm × 6 cm (12 in × 2½ in) strip of felt. Glue on strips of coloured felt for the stripes and pieces of cotton fringing for the ends.

Painted Terracotta Flowerpots

Store your bits and pieces in these colourful pots, or use them to plant bulbs in the spring.

YOU WILL NEED
terracotta flowerpot
coloured paints (acrylic or emulsion)
paintbrushes
varnish (optional)
PVA (white) glue (optional)

paints

flowerpot

varnish

paintbrushes

1 Paint the inside of the flowerpot in a single colour. Allow to dry.

2 Paint the outside rim of the pot in another colour. Allow to dry.

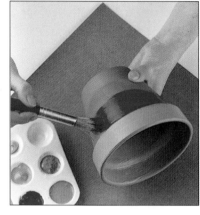

3 Paint the rest of the outside in a third colour.

4 Paint spots on the inside of the pot.

5 Paint stripes on the rim and spots around the rest of the pot and leave it to dry thoroughly.

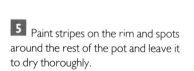

6 Complete the design with more spots. Varnish the pot completely and leave it to dry before using. If you don't want to use varnish, you can use PVA (white) glue thinned with water. Use a paintbrush to cover the pot. It will dry clear, like varnish.

IMPORTANT SAFETY NOTE
Always use varnish in an area where there is plenty of air. Do not breathe in the varnish fumes, and clean your brushes thoroughly afterwards.

Salt Dough Buttons and Beads

Make your own personalized fashion accessories.

YOU WILL NEED
salt dough (see page 16)
toothpick
baking tray (sheet)
oven gloves
fish slice (spatula)
cooling rack
coloured paints
paintbrush
embroidery thread
rolling pin
tracing paper and card (cardboard)
   for templates
pencil
scissors
knife

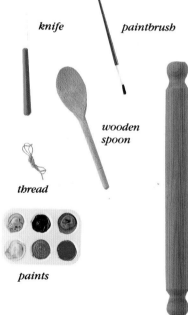

knife *paintbrush*

wooden spoon

rolling pin

thread

paints

1 Make the salt dough following the instructions on page 11. For the beads, mould a small piece of salt dough on the palm of your hand to form either a round, oblong or flat shape.

2 Pierce a hole through the beads with a toothpick. Lay the beads out on a greased baking tray (sheet). With the help of an adult, heat the oven to 100°C/225°F/Gas 2 and put in the baking tray. Cook for approximately 6 hours or until the beads are hard. Wearing oven gloves, remove the baking tray from the oven. With a fish slice (spatula) slide the beads onto a cooling rack. The beads will be very hot. Allow to cool before painting.

3 Paint the beads in lots of different colours and patterns. Allow each coat of paint to dry before adding the next so the colours don't smudge.

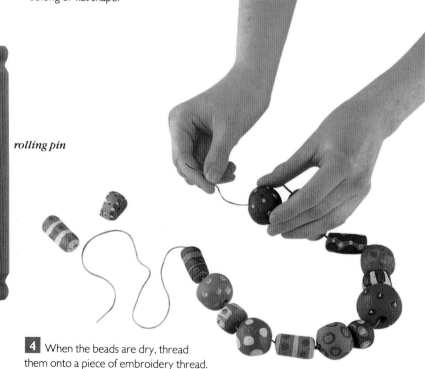

4 When the beads are dry, thread them onto a piece of embroidery thread.

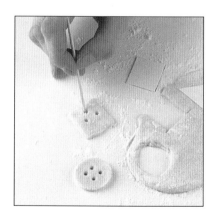

5 For the buttons, sprinkle some flour onto a flat surface and roll out a piece of salt dough until it is 5 mm (¼ in) thick. Trace the templates from the back of the book following the instructions on page 12. Place the templates onto the dough and cut around them with a knife. Pierce 4 holes on each button. Bake them in the oven in the same way as the beads in step 2.

IMPORTANT SAFETY NOTE

You will need an adult to help you to heat the oven and remove the salt dough once it has been baked. Use oven gloves, and do not touch the baking tray (sheet) until it has cooled completely.

6 Paint the buttons when cool and allow to dry. Sew them onto a shirt, cardigan or even a hat. You will have to remove them before washing the clothes. Salt dough should not be washed with water or in a washing machine.

Cress Eggs

These funny eggs have hair that grows. You can give them a haircut and use the 'hair' as a tasty sandwich filling!

YOU WILL NEED
2 eggs
small bowl
cotton wool (ball)
water
cress seeds
coloured paints
paintbrush

cress seeds

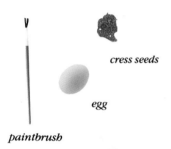

egg

paintbrush

cotton wool (ball)

paints

1 Carefully crack the eggs in half and empty the contents into a small bowl.

2 Moisten a piece of cotton wool (ball) in cold water and place it inside each egg shell half.

3 Sprinkle the cress seeds sparingly onto the cotton wool. Store the egg shells in a dark place for two days or until the seeds have sprouted, then transfer to a light area such as a windowsill.

4 Paint a jolly face onto each egg shell.

Papier-mâché Napkin Ring

Add some colour to the dinner table with fun napkin rings. You can make your own designs for different occasions.

YOU WILL NEED
tracing and plain paper for template
pencil
scissors
card (cardboard)
PVA (white) glue
cardboard toilet roll
masking tape
water
large bowl
newspaper
wooden stick
coloured paints
paintbrush

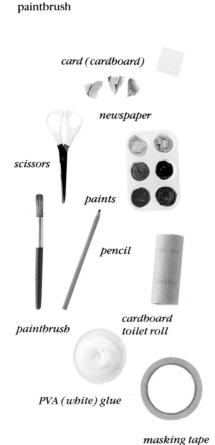

card (cardboard)

newspaper

scissors

paints

paintbrush

pencil

cardboard toilet roll

PVA (white) glue

masking tape

1 Trace the sweet (candy) template from the back of the book following the instructions on page 12. Place the template onto the card (cardboard) and cut it out. Stick the sweets together with PVA (white) glue. Do not stick the tags because they have to be bent outwards.

2 Cut a toilet roll in half and attach the sweet to it with masking tape.

3 For the papier-mâché, mix some glue with water in a large bowl and stir in several layers of torn-up newspaper with a wooden stick. Cover the napkin ring with three layers of papier-mâché and leave to dry overnight in a warm place.

4 When completely dry, paint the napkin ring in an assortment of colours and patterns.

Magic Box

Build your own fantasy world within a box. You could choose any theme you like – a jungle, a circus, or the bottom of the sea, as here.

YOU WILL NEED
coloured paints
paintbrush
cardboard box
scissors
pictures of shells and fish (cut from
    wrapping paper)
PVA (white) glue
netting
blue cellophane
card (cardboard)
pencil
glitter
tracing and plain paper for templates
cotton thread
wooden sticks

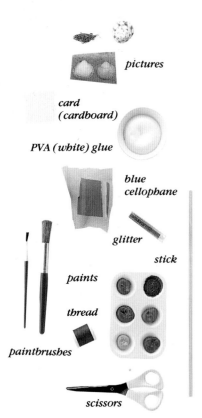

pictures

*card
(cardboard)*

PVA (white) glue

*blue
cellophane*

glitter

stick

paints

thread

paintbrushes

scissors

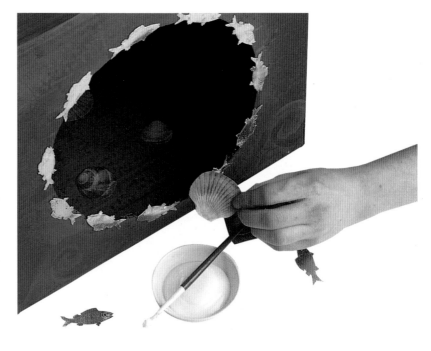

1 Paint the cardboard box both inside and out. Allow to dry. With a pair of scissors, cut out a rectangle from the top of the box and a circle from the front.

2 Decorate the opening with pictures of fish. Decorate the inside of the box with netting and cut-outs of shells stuck down with PVA (white) glue. Glue a piece of blue cellophane to the back wall.

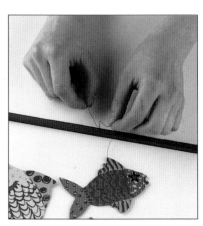

3 Draw a wave onto a piece of card (cardboard) with a pencil. Cut it out and dab on some spots of glue. Sprinkle glitter over the glue and allow to dry. Cover the wave in blue cellophane.

4 Trace the fish and seaweed templates from the back of the book following the instructions on page 12. Place the templates onto a piece of card and cut them out. Paint the shapes in an assortment of colours and leave to dry.

5 Tie a piece of cotton thread to each fish and seaweed shape and tie them to wooden sticks.

CRAFT HINT

If you can't find pictures of shells on wrapping paper look in magazines for pictures. You could also draw your own if you don't find any you like.

6 Place the sticks across the rectangle and dangle the sea-shapes inside the box.

Space Rocket

Travel in time with your very own rocket, made from objects around the house.

YOU WILL NEED
clear plastic bottle
tin foil
scouring pad
scissors
double-sided sticky-tape
shiny paper
PVA (white) glue
paintbrush
tinsel
foil pie dishes (pans)

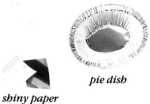

pie dish

shiny paper

sticky-tape

scouring pad

PVA (white) glue

tinsel

scissors

plastic bottle

1 Fill the bottle with scrunched-up pieces of tin foil.

2 Cut the scouring pad in half with a pair of scissors and attach it to the top of the bottle with double-sided sticky-tape. Cut out two spots from the shiny paper and stick onto each side of the pad with PVA (white) glue.

3 Attach a piece of double-sided sticky-tape onto the lid end of the bottle and wrap the tinsel around it.

4 Cut the pie dishes (pans) in half and fold them in half again. Stick to the bottom of the bottle with sticky-tape.

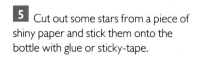

5 Cut out some stars from a piece of shiny paper and stick them onto the bottle with glue or sticky-tape.

6 Cut out two pieces of shiny paper for the wings and glue them onto either side of the bottle.

Painting Eggs

The perfect Easter gift for your friends and family.
Put them in baskets or hide them for an egg hunt.

YOU WILL NEED
eggs
pin
small bowl
coloured paints
paintbrush

egg

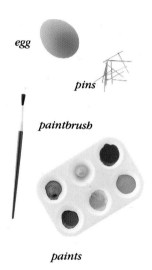

pins

paintbrush

paints

CRAFT HINT

Make a whole batch of eggs in different colours. You could paint on names or paint faces to look like your friends and family.

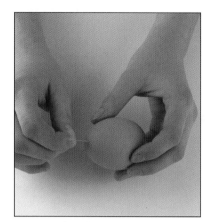

1 Pierce a hole in both ends of each egg with a pin.

2 Carefully blow the contents of the egg into a small bowl.

3 Paint one half of the egg and leave it to dry. Paint the other half in a different colour if you wish.

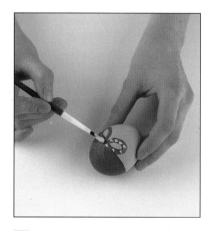

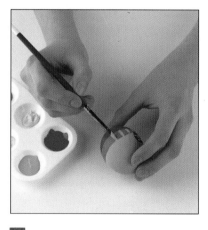

4 When the paint is dry, add a spotty bow.

5 When the bow is dry, paint a band of different colours around the egg.

6 Finish decorating the egg with coloured spots.

Papier-mâché Treasure Box

Keep your favourite treasures hidden away in this box.

YOU WILL NEED
small cardboard box
pencil
scissors
cardboard
PVA (white) glue
paintbrush
tracing and plain paper for template
card (cardboard)
masking tape
water
large bowl
newspaper
wooden stick
coloured paints
foil sweet (candy) wrappers

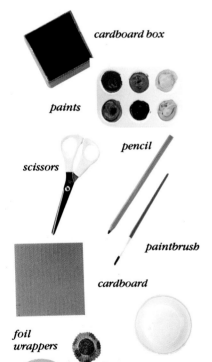

cardboard box
paints
scissors
pencil
paintbrush
cardboard
foil wrappers
PVA (white) glue
newspaper
masking tape

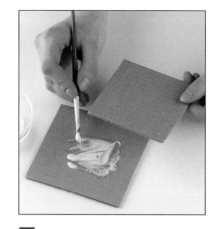

1 For the lid, draw round the box with a pencil on a piece of cardboard and cut it out with a pair of scissors. Cut out a slightly smaller piece and stick this onto the slightly larger piece with PVA (white) glue. Leave to dry.

2 Trace the jewel template from the back of the book following the instructions on page 12. Place the template onto the card (cardboard) and cut it out. Bend along the marked lines to join the jewel together and fasten with masking tape.

3 Glue one of the jewel's triangular sides onto the lid.

4 For the papier-mâché, mix some glue with water in a large bowl and stir in several layers of torn-up newspaper with a wooden stick. Apply three layers of papier-mâché to the box and the lid and allow them to dry overnight in a warm place. (This may take a little longer depending on the time of year.)

5 When the box is completely dry, paint the inside and the outside of both the box and the lid. Allow to dry.

6 Flatten the sweet (candy) wrappers and cut out circles from them. Glue the circles onto the box as decoration.

Musical Instrument

Discover your musical talents with this fun, colourful instrument. You can pluck the string and run the stick over the corrugated paper. You can even hit the top or sides like a drum.

YOU WILL NEED
plain and shiny corrugated paper
cardboard box
PVA (white) glue
felt-tip pen
scissors
coloured paints
paintbrush
tinsel
double-sided sticky-tape
wooden broom pole
coloured sticky-tape
string

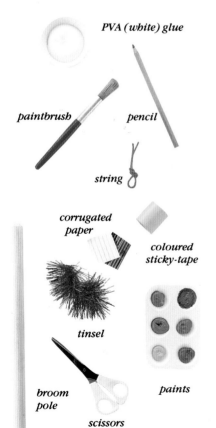

PVA (white) glue

paintbrush   pencil

string

corrugated
paper

coloured
sticky-tape

tinsel

broom
pole   paints

scissors

1 Stick a piece of corrugated paper around the upright sides of the cardboard box with PVA (white) glue.

2 With a felt-tip pen, draw a circle on one side of the box and carefully cut it out with scissors to make a hole.

3 Glue a piece of shiny corrugated paper on the top of the box. Paint the rest of the box a bright colour.

4 Stick the tinsel around the hole using either glue or double-sided sticky-tape.

5 Paint the wooden broom pole and attach it to the side of the box using coloured sticky-tape.

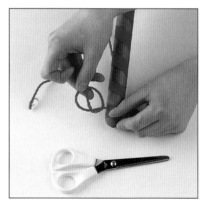

6 Thread the string through the hole at the top of the pole and tie a knot. Make a hole at the top and bottom of the box and thread the string through. Tie a knot to secure. It will need to be very tight to make a noise.

Natural Christmas Decorations

In ancient times people in Europe worshipped many different gods of nature. Holly, ivy, mistletoe, yew and other plants held religious meaning for these people. Memories have been passed down with our folklore. Today, these plants are still used to decorate homes at Christmas.

YOU WILL NEED
Christmas greenery
newspaper
dried seed heads
pine cones
gold and silver spray paint
florist's foam for flower arranging
candles
red berries
Christmas tree decorations
ribbon
sticky tape
string
wire
tinsel

spray paint

candle   *florist's foam*

string

tinsel

1 Gather together some greenery such as holly, ivy, mistletoe, conifer sprigs and other evergreen leaves.

2 Spread out the newspaper in a well ventilated area. Spray dried seed heads and pine cones with gold or silver paint. Allow to dry before using as decorations.

3 To make a table decoration, stick greenery into florists' foam.

4 Push a candle into the middle of the foam. Decorate with sprayed seed heads, cones, berries, Christmas tree decorations and tinsel.

5 To make a Christmas wreath, tape or tie greenery around a circle of wire, cane or twigs.

6 Decorate with pine cones and ribbons and other pretty objects. Look at the picture opposite. Can you see some other ideas for natural Christmas decorations?

Christmas Stocking

Hang this stocking at the end of your bed for Santa to fill with plenty of Christmas presents.

YOU WILL NEED
paper
pencil
scissors
colourful or patterned fabric
red felt
needle
thread
pins
velvet ribbon
rik-rak braid
PVA (white) glue
paintbrush
buttons

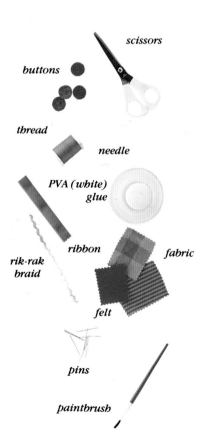

scissors

buttons

thread

needle

PVA (white) glue

ribbon

rik-rak braid

fabric

felt

pins

paintbrush

1 Draw a stocking shape on a piece of paper, and use it as a pattern. You will need to make the pattern 1 cm (½ in) bigger all around to allow for the seam. Cut out 2 pieces of fabric for the main part of the stocking. Cut out a spiky border from red felt for the top.

2 Fold over the top edge of each stocking piece and sew with a needle and thread.

3 Pin the two stocking pieces together making sure the right sides are facing each other. Sew around the bottom and sides leaving a 1 cm (½ in) seam allowance. Turn the stocking right-side out.

4 Pin the red spiky felt around the top edge of the stocking together with a piece of velvet ribbon for the loop, and sew.

5 Stick some more velvet ribbon and some rik-rak braid onto the red felt with PVA (white) glue.

6 Sew some buttons onto the red felt.

IMPORTANT SAFETY NOTE

You may need an adult's help for the sewing. If you don't want to sew, you could make the entire stocking from felt, and glue the sides together with a thin layer of PVA (white) glue.

DRESSING-UP FUN

Making a Waistband

Elasticated waistbands make all costumes easy to put on and take off.

YOU WILL NEED
needle and thread or sewing machine
safety pin
elastic

1 Fold over the waist and sew a line of stitches to make a tube. Leave a gap to thread the elastic through.

2 Attach a safety pin to the end of the elastic and thread it through the tube until it comes out the other end.

3 Pull the two ends of elastic to gather the waist to the right size and tie a knot. Sew up the opening in the tube.

Covering a Button

By covering buttons you can choose your own fabric to match the outfit. The clown costume includes lots of colourful buttons.

YOU WILL NEED
fabric
scissors
self-covering button
needle and thread

1 Cut out a circle of fabric twice as wide as the button. Sew a line of running stitches around the edge of circle.

2 Open the button and place the front on the circle of fabric. Pull the threads to gather them up around the button.

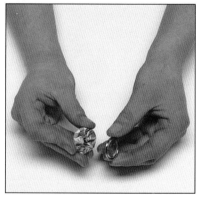

3 Place the back on the button.

Decorative Stitches

These stitches can add a finishing touch to an outfit, whether adding colourful details in thread, or sewing on fabric shapes.

YOU WILL NEED
needle and thread

1 Running stitch is useful for sewing on patches and other shapes. You can make the stitches as long or as short as you like.

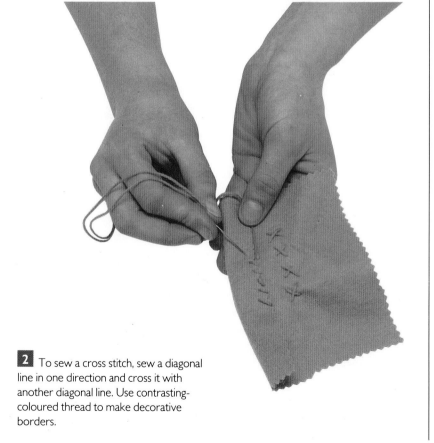

2 To sew a cross stitch, sew a diagonal line in one direction and cross it with another diagonal line. Use contrasting-coloured thread to make decorative borders.

Making your own Pantaloons

Decorate the pantaloons according to the character required. These basic pantaloons can be used for the genie costume.

YOU WILL NEED
2 metres/2 yards fabric
pattern, enlarged from the template section
scissors
needle and thread or sewing machine
safety pin
elastic

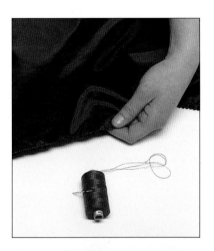

1 Fold the fabric in half, with the right sides facing, and place the pattern on the fold of the fabric. Cut out two identical pieces. Keep each piece of the pantaloon folded in half with the right sides facing and sew along the inside leg with a 5 mm/¼ in seam allowance.

2 Turn one leg piece right side out and place it inside the other leg, matching up the raw edges. Stitch the two pieces together. Turn the legs right side out. Fold over the waist of the pantaloons and sew a double line of stitching to make a tube for the elastic to go through. Leave a gap to thread the elastic through. Do the same around the bottom of each pantaloon leg.

3 Attach the safety pin to one end of the elastic and tie a knot at the end. Thread the elastic through the tube. Do the same with each pantaloon leg. Sew up the gaps in the tubes.

Making a Tail

This tail was made to go with the spotted dog outfit. You can make a tail for a cat or tiger in the same way.

YOU WILL NEED
old pair of children's black tights
scissors
newspaper
elastic
needle and thread
felt
fabric glue

newspaper

fabric glue

scissors

tights

1 Cut one leg off the pair of tights. Scrunch up balls of newspaper and fill up the leg until it is quite firm.

2 Tie a knot at the end of the leg.

3 Measure your waist so you know how much elastic you need. Sew the elastic in a loop onto the knotted end of the tail.

4 This tail is for the spotted dog so it has been decorated with spots of felt glued on with fabric glue. You could always paint on a different design using fabric paints.

Making Ears

These ears add a cuddly touch to any of the animal outfits. You can adjust the size of the ears and choose material to suit the animal.

YOU WILL NEED
hairband
tape measure
fake fur
scissors
needle and thread
felt
fabric glue (optional)
template for ears
cardboard
pencil

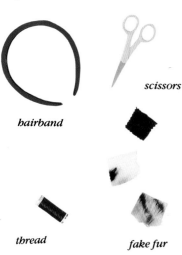

hairband

scissors

thread

fake fur

1 Measure the length of the hairband with a tape measure. Cut out a piece of fur to fit, allowing an extra 2 cm/1 in at each end for folding over. Sew the fur onto the hairband as shown.

2 Cut out a piece of felt to fit the inside of the hairband and sew or glue it on.

3 Trace the appropriate template from the back of the book onto a piece of cardboard and draw around the cardboard on the reverse side of the fur. You will need two pieces of fur for each ear. Place the two pieces of fur together with the right sides facing and sew round, leaving a gap to turn the right sides out.

4 Sew the ears onto the hairband, making sure they are in the correct position.

Cat

Use the instructions given previously in this chapter to make a pair of black furry ears. Dress up in a black catsuit and you will be the most glamorous, sleek pussy cat in town.

YOU WILL NEED
make-up sponge
water-based face paints
medium make-up brush
fine make-up brush
thick make-up brush
blusher

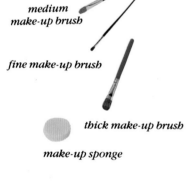

*medium
make-up brush*

fine make-up brush

thick make-up brush

make-up sponge

water-based face paints

1 Using a damp sponge, apply a white base over the whole face. Using a medium brush, paint a border of black spikes around the edge of the face. You might find it easier to paint the outline first and then fill it in.

2 Paint a black outline around the eyes as shown and paint over the eyebrows.

3 Making sure the model's eyes are closed, fill in the eyelids and inside the black outline with a bright colour. This is a very delicate part of the face, so take care, and do not apply make-up too close to the eyelashes. Paint above the eyes.

4 Using a fine brush, paint a heart shape on the tip of the nose and a thin line joining the nose to the chin, avoiding the mouth.

5 Paint the lips a bright colour and paint black whisker spots under the nose

6 Using a thick brush, dust each cheek with blusher.

Mouse

Use the template and the instructions provided earlier to make a pair of furry mouse ears. Beware of cats and owls when you are wearing this costume as one of their favourite meals is little mice!

YOU WILL NEED
make-up sponge
water-based face paints
black make-up (eye-liner) pencil
medium make-up brush
thick make-up brush
pink blusher
fine make-up brush

make-up sponge

water-based face paints

fine make-up brush

medium make-up brush

thick make-up brush

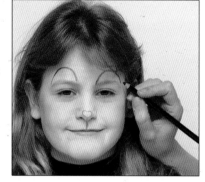

1 Using a damp sponge, apply a base coat of white over the face. With a black make-up (eye-liner) pencil, mark a pair of eyebrows above the model's own. Draw the outline of a heart on the tip of the nose and draw a line joining the nose to the mouth.

2 Using a medium brush, paint the area under the drawn eyebrows white. Apply more white underneath the model's eyes. Paint the heart pink and the outlines of the eyebrows and the heart black. Paint a line that joins the nose to the mouth and continue the line onto the centre of the top lip, forming a triangle.

3 Using a thick brush, dust pink blusher onto each cheek.

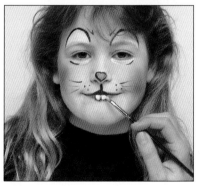

4 Using a fine brush, paint the black outline of the teeth over the bottom lip. Fill in the teeth white. Paint on a few black whisker spots and whiskers.

Panda

If you only have a few face paints, this is the perfect project for you. It is good for beginners as it is simple to do. Use the template and the instructions provided earlier to make a pair of furry ears to match.

YOU WILL NEED
black make-up (eye-liner) pencil
make-up sponge
water-based face paints
medium make-up brush
fine make-up brush

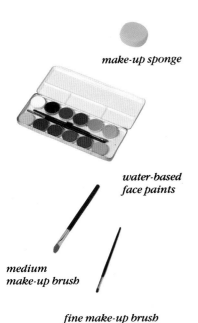

make-up sponge

*water-based
face paints*

*medium
make-up brush*

fine make-up brush

1 Using a black make-up (eye-liner) pencil, gently draw an outline around each eye as shown. Draw an outline across the tip of the nose.

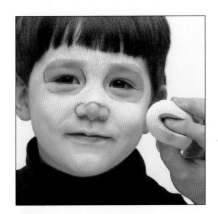

2 Using a damp sponge, apply a white base over the face, avoiding the areas you have just marked with the pencil.

3 Using a medium brush, paint the eyes and the tip of the nose black. Using a fine brush, paint a line joining the nose to the mouth and paint the lips. Paint small whisker spots either side of the mouth. Add black lines between the eyebrows.

Tiger

For a complete look, dress up in an outfit made from fake tiger fur and use the instructions at the beginning of this chapter to make a pair of matching furry ears.

YOU WILL NEED
make-up sponge
water-based face paints
medium make-up brush
fine make-up brush

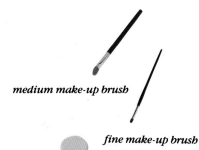

medium make-up brush

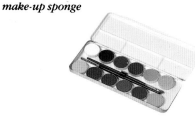

fine make-up brush

make-up sponge

water-based face paints

1 Using a damp sponge, apply the base colour over the face.

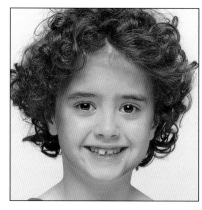

2 Rinse the sponge, then stipple a darker shade of paint around the edge of the face as shown.

3 Sponge the chin and the area above the mouth white. Using a medium brush, paint the area around the eyes white as shown. You might find it easier to paint the outline first and then fill it in.

4 Using a medium brush, paint on the black markings around each eye, as shown, making sure each side is the same.

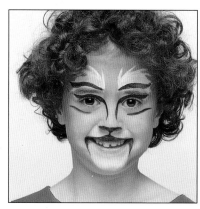

5 Using a fine brush, paint the tip of the nose black and paint a thin black line from the centre of the nose to the top lip. Paint the top lip black and extend the line at each corner of the mouth, stopping half-way down the chin.

6 For the rest of the markings, paint brushstrokes of colour across the face. To keep the design symmetrical, finish one side of the face first and then copy the design onto the other side.

Spotted Dog

This funny dog's outfit is easy to make. Simply cut out circles of felt and stick them onto a pair of leggings and a T-shirt using fabric glue. Use the template and the instructions provided earlier to make a pair of spotted ears and a tail to match.

YOU WILL NEED
make-up sponge
water-based face paints
fine make-up brush
medium make-up brush

make-up sponge

water-based face paints

fine make-up brush

medium make-up brush

1 Using a damp sponge, apply a white base colour over the face. Gently sponge a slightly darker shade around the eyes.

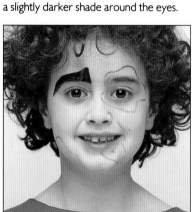

2 Paint one eyebrow black and, using a fine make-up brush, paint a wiggly outline around the other eye to make a patch. Paint another patch outline on the side of the face. Paint the outline for a droopy tongue below the bottom lip.

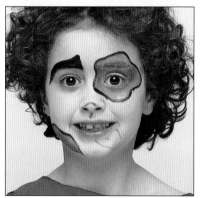

3 Using a medium brush fill in the patches grey and outline them in black. Draw the outline for the nose and a line joining the nose to the mouth.

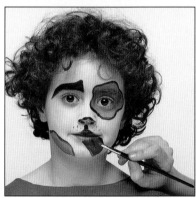

4 Fill in the tongue red and outline in black. Paint a short black line along the centre of the tongue. Fill in the tip of the nose pink and add a thick black line where the nose joins the mouth. Paint the centre of the top lip black. Paint black whisker spots under the nose.

Rabbit

This adorable little bunny is dressed all in white. As well as using the instructions provided earlier to make a pair of furry ears, you could also make a fluffy tail from cotton wool and stick it onto the T-shirt.

YOU WILL NEED
make-up sponge
water-based face paints
black make-up (eye-liner) pencil
medium make-up brush
pink blusher (optional)
fine make-up brush

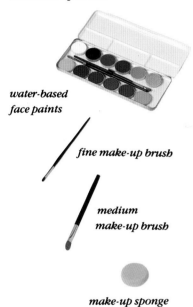

*water-based
face paints*

fine make-up brush

*medium
make-up brush*

make-up sponge

1 Using a damp sponge, apply a white base over the face.

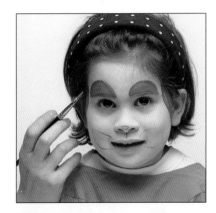

2 Using a black make-up (eye-liner) pencil draw a heart on the tip of the nose, a circular outline above each eyebrow, a line joining the nose to the mouth and a circle on each cheek. Using a medium brush, fill in the marked area above the eyebrows grey.

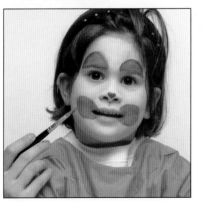

3 Paint the heart at the tip of the nose red and paint the cheeks pink with water-based face paints or pink blusher.

4 Using a fine brush, draw the outline of the teeth over the bottom lip and fill them in with white make-up. Using a medium brush, paint the line joining the nose to the mouth black. Paint black whiskers above each eyebrow and on each cheek.

Bumble Bee

Buzz around in this striped outfit. Why not paint a pair of tights or leggings in the same style?

YOU WILL NEED
yellow T-shirt
newspaper
black fabric paint
paintbrush
paints
hairband
paper baubles (balls)
scissors
milliner's wire
needle and thread
black felt
glue
black cardboard
pencil
needle and thread

FOR THE FACE
make-up sponge
water-based face paints
medium make-up brush

hairband

fabric paint

paints

medium make-up brush

glue

1 Place the T-shirt on a flat, well-covered surface. Fill the T-shirt with flat pieces of newspaper. Paint black lines across the T-shirt and on the arms and leave the paint to dry. Turn the T-shirt over to the other side and continue painting the lines.

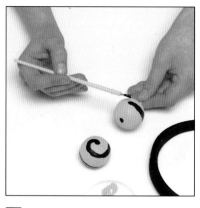

2 For the antennae, first paint the hairband black and leave the paint to dry. Paint the paper baubles (balls) yellow and, when the paint has dried, paint a black line around each one.

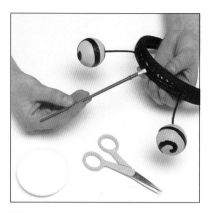

3 Cut a length of wire, approximately 45 cm/18 in long. Bend the wire to fit the hairband, making sure each piece of wire that will support the bauble is the same length. Sew the wire onto the hairband and glue a strip of black felt over the wire for extra support. Secure the baubles onto the ends of the wire.

4 Fold a piece of black cardboard in half and draw the shape of a wing, so that, when it is cut out and the paper is opened out, you will have two identical wings that are joined together. Sew the wings along the fold onto the back of the T-shirt.

5 For the face, use a damp sponge to apply a yellow base. Using a medium brush, paint a black line on the eyelids and under each eye. Paint a black spot on the tip of the nose.

Dinosaur

Dress up as a prehistoric monster in this spiky camouflaged outfit.

YOU WILL NEED
green fabric or felt
scissors
green polo neck (turtleneck) or
    T-shirt
fabric glue
needle and thread
fire resistant stuffing (batting)
hairband
green paint
paintbrush
glue

FOR THE FACE
make-up sponge
water-based face paints
stipple sponge
medium make-up brush

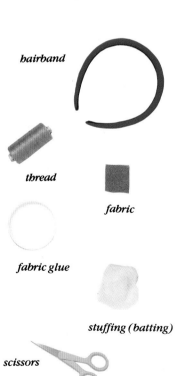

hairband

thread

fabric

fabric glue

stuffing (batting)

scissors

1 To make the costume, cut out lots of triangles, more or less the same size, from a piece of old green fabric or felt. You could use different coloured green fabrics if you don't have enough of one kind.

2 Starting at the bottom of the shirt, glue on the fabric spikes so that they overlap each other. Leave a circle in the centre of the shirt empty.

3 For each spike on the spine, you will need to cut out two triangles. Sew the two triangles together with right sides facing. Turn the triangles right side out and fill with stuffing (batting) to make a spike shape. Sew a running stitch around the bottom edge of the spike and pull gently. This will draw up the threads and close the spike. Tie a knot.

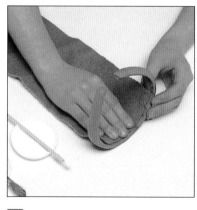

4 Paint the hairband green and leave it to dry. Cut a strip of green fabric approximately 10 cm/4 in wide and however long you wish it to be. Using glue, secure the strip onto the inside of the hairband and leave to dry.

5 Sew the spikes onto the strip of fabric attached to the hairband.

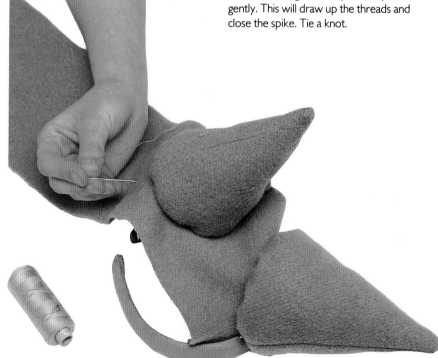

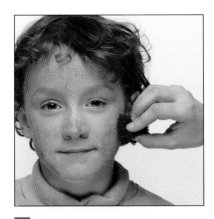

6 For the face, use a damp sponge to apply the base colour over the face. Using a stipple sponge, dab a darker shade over the base colour.

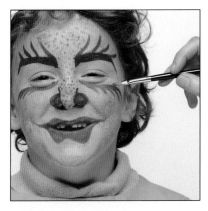

7 Using a medium brush, decorate the face. Paint on wild eyebrows, exaggerated nostrils, spots, big lips and markings under each eye.

Clown

Bounce around in this jolly outfit and entertain your friends and family. Decorate a hat and an old pair of shoes to match the colourful costume.

YOU WILL NEED
6 self-covering buttons
scraps of fabric
template for clown button
pencil
coloured felt
scissors
needle and thread
old shirt
old pair of trousers (pants)
fabric glue
milliner's wire
broad ribbon
fabric for the bow tie
narrow ribbon

FOR THE FACE
make-up sponge
water-based face paints
black make-up (eye-liner) pencil
medium make-up brush
fine make-up brush
thick make-up brush

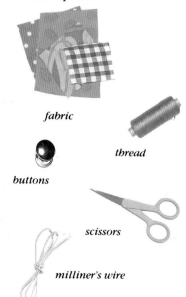

fabric

thread

buttons

scissors

milliner's wire

1 To make the costume, cover each button in a different scrap of fabric. Using the template, draw and cut out a flower shape from a piece of felt and snip a hole in the centre of it. Fix the flower onto the back of the button and secure on the back. Sew the buttons onto the shirt and trousers (pants).

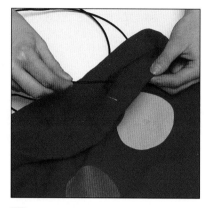

2 Cut out large dots of felt and stick them onto the trousers with fabric glue. Thread a piece of milliner's wire through the waistband. Twist the two ends of the wire together to secure them.

3 Sew two separate lengths of ribbon onto the waist of the trousers to make a pair of braces (suspenders). Sew a covered button onto each brace.

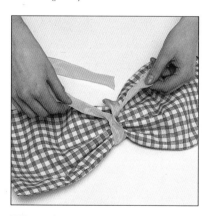

4 To make the bow tie, sew two rectangular pieces of fabric together with the right sides facing, leaving a gap. Turn right side out and stitch the gap. Tie a piece of ribbon around the centre of the rectangle and tie a knot. Tie around the clown's neck under the shirt collar.

5 For the face, use a damp sponge to apply a smooth white base.

6 Using a black make-up (eye-liner) pencil, draw the outline of a clown's mouth. Draw a pair of eyebrows above the model's own and gently mark an area around each eye as shown.

7 Using a medium brush, paint the area around each eye with lots of colour and paint over the drawn eyebrows with a thick black line.

8 Using a fine brush, paint the mouth red, and outline the shape of the mouth in black. Using a thick brush, colour the cheeks a rosy red.

Ballerina

Show off your ballet steps in this pretty tutu. Make it the same colour as your ballet leotard.

YOU WILL NEED
2 metres/2 yards coloured netting
needle, thread and pins
tape measure
wide ribbon for the waistband
narrow ribbon for the bows
scissors
matching leotard and tights

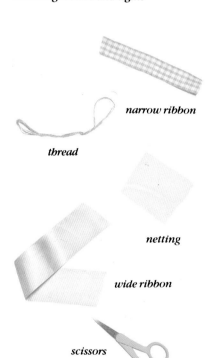

narrow ribbon

thread

netting

wide ribbon

scissors

1 Fold the netting over lengthwise and sew a line of running stitch along the folded edge. Measure your ballerina's waist. For a short tutu, fold over again, and secure with running stitches. Pull the thread gently to gather the netting to fit the waist and tie a knot or sew a few stitches to secure the gathers.

2 Pin the wide ribbon onto the gathered netting and then sew it on.

3 Using the narrower ribbon, tie approximately six small bows. Sew five bows onto the waistband.

4 To finish the costume, sew the last bow onto the leotard.

Fairy

Dress up in this sparkling outfit and make a special wish. For a magical effect, wear a white leotard and pin some tinsel in your hair.

YOU WILL NEED
2 metres/2 yards netting
needle and thread
scissors
tinsel
1.5 metres/1½ yards white fabric
milliner's wire
silver elastic cord
garden cane
silver paint
paintbrush
silver paper or cardboard
adhesive tape
glue
white leotard and tights

paintbrush

milliner's wire

garden cane

fabric

tinsel

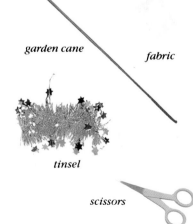

scissors

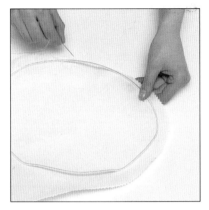

1 To make the tutu, follow the instructions for the ballerina tutu, folding the netting lengthwise once only for a longer skirt. Instead of decorating the waistband with ribbon, sew on a piece of tinsel. Cut out two pieces of white fabric for the wings, in a figure-of-eight shape. On the wrong side of one of the pieces of fabric, sew a separate length of wire around each wing.

2 Place the other piece of fabric on top of the first, making sure the wrong sides are facing. Sew around the edge to secure the two pieces together.

3 Sew a loop of elastic cord onto each wing, near the centre. These will slip over the arms to support the wings on the body.

4 To make the wand, first paint a garden cane silver and leave it to dry. Cut out two silver stars and fasten the silver stick onto the reverse side of one of the stars with a piece of adhesive tape. Glue the stars together.

Scarecrow

If you don't have any suitable old clothes of your own, visit a second-hand clothes shop or rummage through piles of clothes at a local flea market. The older the clothes are the better the costume will be.

YOU WILL NEED
raffia
old felt hat
scissors
plastic toy mouse
glue
needle and thread
old clothes, such as a jacket and
    trousers (pants)
scraps of fabric
orange cardboard
orange paint
paintbrush
elastic cord

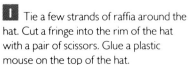
fabric

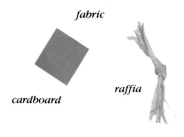
cardboard

raffia

scissors

paint

1 Tie a few strands of raffia around the hat. Cut a fringe into the rim of the hat with a pair of scissors. Glue a plastic mouse on the top of the hat.

2 Tie bundles of raffia in a knot and sew the bundles around the inside rim of the hat, leaving a gap at the front.

3 Cut ragged edges on the jacket and the trousers (pants).

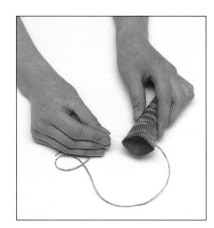

4 Cut scraps of fabric into squares and rectangles and sew them onto the jacket and the trousers.

5 To make the nose, cut a piece of orange cardboard into a cone shape. Roll the cardboard into a cone and glue it together.

6 Paint orange lines around the cone and leave them to dry. Make a small hole on either side of the cone and thread a piece of elastic cord through that will fit around your head. Tie a knot at each end of the elastic.

Gypsy

Wear your brightest clothes to go with the accessories and make up your own gypsy dance.

YOU WILL NEED
cardboard
scissors
newspaper
PVA (white) glue
bowl
water
paints
paintbrush
glitter
sequins
fabric for the head scarf and shawl
needle and thread or sewing machine
braid
pom-poms

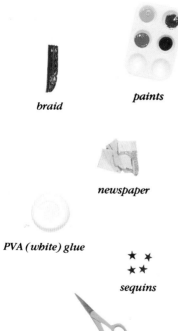

braid

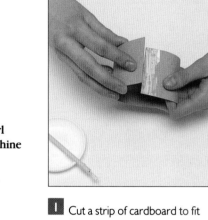

paints

newspaper

PVA (white) glue

sequins

scissors

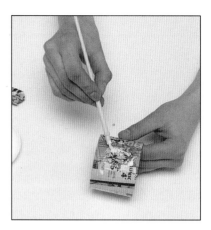

1 Cut a strip of cardboard to fit comfortably around your wrist and approximately 5 cm/2 in wide. Bend the cardboard to make a bracelet and glue it in place.

2 Scrunch up small balls of newspaper and glue them onto the bracelet. Cover the bangle in three layers of papier mâché as described in the introduction, and leave it to dry thoroughly in a warm place.

3 Paint the bangle using lots of colours and leave the paint to dry.

4 Paint dabs of glue on the bangle and sprinkle on the glitter. Glue a few sequins on for extra sparkle and decoration. Leave the glue to dry before trying on the bracelet.

5 For the head scarf, sew two triangular pieces of fabric together with the right sides facing. Leave a gap and turn right side out. Sew up the gap.

6 Sew a strip of braid along the longest side of the scarf. Make a larger, but similar, scarf to go around the neck and sew pom-poms along the sides.

Cowboy

Find a hat and a toy gun to complete this costume.
Round up your friends and have fun.

YOU WILL NEED
tape measure
felt for the waistcoat (vest)
scissors
needle and thread or sewing machine
templates for pocket
pins
fabric glue
template for sheriff badge
pencil
cardboard
tin foil or silver paint
paintbrush
safety pin
strong adhesive tape

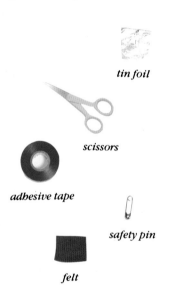

tin foil

scissors

adhesive tape

safety pin

felt

1 For the waistcoat (vest), measure from the nape of your neck to the length required, and cut two squares of felt to this size. Cut one piece in half lengthways for the two front pieces. With the right sides facing, sew the two front pieces to the back along the shoulders. Sew the sides together leaving gaps for the arms.

2 Turn the waistcoat right side out. Use the template to cut out two pockets from felt. Pin them in position on the front. Use the template to cut out two pieces of fabric in a contrasting colour to decorate the top of each pocket and glue them on with fabric glue. Sew the pockets onto the waistcoat using brightly coloured thread.

3 Using a pair of scissors, snip along the bottom of the waistcoat to make a fringe.

4 To make the badge, draw around the template and cut out a piece of cardboard. Cover it in tin foil or paint it silver. Decorate the badge with a silver 'S' in the centre and silver spots on the tip of each point. Fasten a safety pin onto the reverse of the badge with a piece of tape.

Knight

Have a pretend battle with your friends in this shiny
suit of armour.

YOU WILL NEED
cardboard
scissors
tin foil
black felt
glue
coloured foil paper
template for helmet
pencil
silver paint
paintbrush
template for body shield
hole puncher
ribbon

paint

glue

scissors

coloured foil paper

tin foil

1 Cut a piece of cardboard in the
shape of a sword. Cover the blade in
silver foil. Cut two pieces of felt to fit the
handle of the sword and glue them on.
Decorate the handle with diamond
shapes cut out of foil paper.

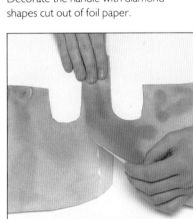

2 To make the helmet, use the
template to draw and cut two equal
pieces of cardboard. Paint these silver and
leave to dry. Glue the two pieces
together as shown in the picture.

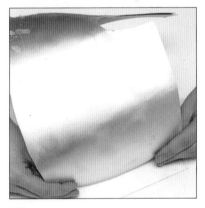

3 When the glue has dried, fold the
helmet so that it curves and glue the sides
together. Hold the helmet together while
the glue dries. To make the body shield
you will need to draw round the shape,
then flip it to complete the other half. Do
this for the front and back pieces and cut
them out.

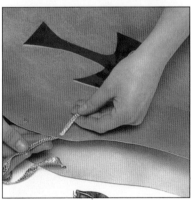

4 Paint the two pieces silver. When the
paint has dried, glue the two pieces
together at the shoulder seam. Cut a foil
paper cross and glue it onto the front of
the shield. Punch a hole on either side of
the body shield and thread a piece of
ribbon through. Tie a knot to secure.

Genie

You can make your own baggy pantaloons by
following the instructions provided.

YOU WILL NEED
pair of shoes
glitter paint
paintbrush
glue
glittery braid
scraps of fabric
baggy trousers (pants) or pantaloons
scissors
fabric glue
fabric for the cummerbund
tape measure
needle and thread or sewing machine
fabric for the turban
feathers

FOR THE FACE
make-up sponge
water-based face paints
medium make-up brush

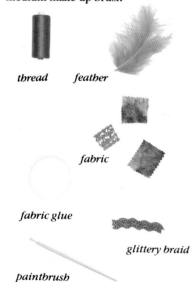

thread   *feather*

fabric

fabric glue

glittery braid

paintbrush

scissors

1 To make the costume, paint a pair of shoes a sparkling colour and leave to dry. Stick a piece of glittery braid around the side of each shoe.

2 Making use of scraps of fabric, cut out lots of stars and glue them onto a pair of baggy trousers (pants) or pantaloons using fabric glue.

3 Measure your waist for the cummerbund, allowing an extra 25 cm/10 in so you can tie the fabric at the back. Sew two pieces of fabric together to the required length with the right sides facing, leaving an opening at one end, and turn it right side out. Sew up the end.

4 Cut out some more stars from scraps of fabric and glue them onto the cummerbund with fabric glue.

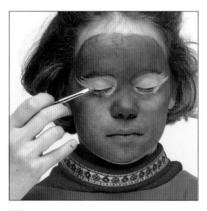

5 For the face, use a damp sponge to apply the base colour, avoiding the area around the eyes. Paint the area around the eyes a bright colour.

6 Tie the turban around the head, tying a knot on the top of the head. Tuck the loose fabric underneath the turban. Place a few colourful feathers on the top of the turban to decorate.

Robot

The fun part of this project is collecting all the bits and pieces to recycle. Ask your friends and family to help you collect interesting boxes, cartons and packages.

YOU WILL NEED
2 cardboard boxes
pencil
scissors
silver spray paint
cartons and containers made of
    cardboard and clear plastic
glue
3 Christmas baubles (balls)
foil pie-dishes (pans)
masking tape
pair of old shoes
2 metal kitchen scourers
tin foil

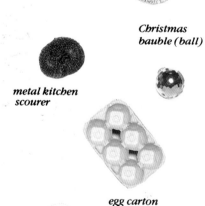

foil pie-dish (pan)

Christmas bauble (ball)

metal kitchen scourer

egg carton

glue

silver spray

scissors

1 To make the helmet you will need a cardboard box that fits comfortably over your head. Draw a square on one side of the box and cut it out.

2 Ask an adult to help spray the box silver. You should do this outdoors or in a very airy room where the surfaces are well covered and protected. When the paint has dried, glue a clear plastic carton over the square hole. Punch a few holes in the carton to let air through.

3 Decorate the box by gluing on Christmas baubles (balls) and foil pie-dishes (pans).

4 For the body of the robot, you will need a large cardboard box. Draw and cut out a hole on the top of the box for your head and one on either side for your arms. Secure the edges of the holes with masking tape.

5 Decorate the robot body by gluing on all the boxes and containers you have been collecting. When the glue has dried, spray the box silver, following the same instructions as in step 2. Leave the paint to dry thoroughly before you try on the costume.

6 Spray a pair of old shoes silver and decorate them with a metal kitchen scourer or anything shiny. Finally, when you are dressed in your costume, ask a friend to wrap your arms and legs in tin foil to finish.

Witch

This young witch looks like she's got a few tricks up her sleeve. She is wearing a cloak made from an old piece of fabric and long black nails.

YOU WILL NEED
tape measure
black fabric for hat
iron-on interfacing (optional)
pencil
scissors
needle and thread
raffia or straw

FOR THE FACE
make-up sponge
water-based face paints
lipstick brush
fine make-up brush
thick make-up brush

black fabric

thread

raffia

iron-on interfacing

scissors

1 To make the hat, measure the width of your head so that you know how wide to make the rim of the hat. If the fabric you are using needs to be stiffened, iron a piece of interfacing onto the reverse side. Ask an adult to help you. Draw and cut out a triangle with a curved base, making sure the rim measures the width of your head with a small allowance for sewing the fabric together.

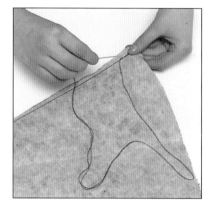

2 With the right sides facing, fold the triangle in half to form a tall cone and sew along the side.

3 Make bundles of raffia or straw and tie a knot in the centre of each bundle. Sew each bundle around the rim of the hat leaving a gap at the front. The more bundles you sew on, the wilder the wig will be. Turn the hat the right way out.

4 For the face, use a damp sponge to dab the base colours over the face.

5 Using a lipstick brush, paint on a pair of wild, black eyebrows. Paint a black line on each eyelid just above the eyelashes. Paint a line of red just under each eye and a black curve below it.

6 Add ageing lines with a fine brush Build more colour onto the cheeks using a thick make-up brush. Paint the lips red, exaggerating the top lip.

Vampire

Dress all in black for this costume. Don't be surprised if you frighten your friends and family with your haunted face.

YOU WILL NEED
make-up sponge
water-based face paints
medium make-up brush
fine make-up brush
black make-up (eyeliner) pencil
   (optional)
red make-up (eyeliner) pencil
fake blood (optional)

water-based face paints

fake blood

fine make-up brush

medium make-up brush

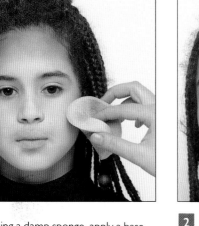

1 Using a damp sponge, apply a base colour on the face. Rinse the sponge, then dab a slightly darker shade on the forehead, blending it with the base colour.

2 Using a medium brush, paint a triangle in the centre of the forehead, one on either side of the face at the cheekbones and a small one at the bottom of the chin. You might find it easier to draw the outline for each shape first, to make sure they are symmetrical, and then fill them in.

3 Using a fine brush paint a pair of jagged eyebrows over the model's own. Again, you may find it easier to draw the outline first.

4 Paint the eyelids white and the area up to the eyebrows grey. Use the red make-up pencil to colour the area under the eyes.

5 Exaggerate the points on the top lip and colour the lips black.

6 Paint the outline of long, pointed fangs under the bottom lip and fill them in with yellow. Dab fake blood or red make-up at the points of the fangs and at the corners of the eyes

Wizard

Wave the magic wand and conjure up some secret spells. Look in flea markets for a piece of material to make the cape.

YOU WILL NEED
tape measure
fabric for hat
fabric interfacing (optional)
scissors
needle and thread
silver fabric
fabric glue
templates for wizard's pendant
pencil
cardboard
tin foil
silver ribbon
double-sided adhesive tape
garden cane
paint
paintbrush
tinsel

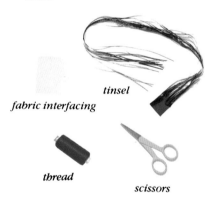

tinsel

fabric interfacing

thread

scissors

1 Measure the width of your head with a tape measure so that you know how wide to make the rim of the hat. If the fabric you are using needs to be stiffened, iron a piece of interfacing onto the reverse side. Ask an adult to help you. Draw and cut out a triangle with a curved base, making sure the rim measures the width of your head with a small allowance for sewing together. Hem the bottom and, with right sides facing, fold the triangle in half to make a tall cone. Sew along the side. Turn the hat the right side out and decorate with silver fabric stars, stuck on with fabric glue.

2 To make the pendant, use the template to cut out a cardboard star. Cut two circles of cardboard of the same size to make the backing. Cover both circles and the star with tin foil. Attach the ribbon to the back of the card circles with a piece of adhesive tape.

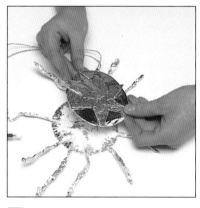

3 Roll up strips of foil and place them on the reverse of one of the foil circles. Glue the other circle on top to trap the foil strips and secure them in place.

4 To make the wand, first paint a garden cane and leave it to dry. Stick a piece of shiny tinsel around one end of the stick with adhesive tape.

Native American

You can buy the feathers for this costume from most good fabric shops. You can make the skirt from felt with an elastic waistband.

YOU WILL NEED
tape measure
wide ribbon
scissors
feathers
felt
fabric glue
needle and embroidery threads
wool
narrow ribbon

FOR THE FACE
water-based face paints
medium make-up brush

feather

thread

felt

fabric glue

scissors

ribbon

1 Measure around your head with a tape measure, allowing a 5 cm/2 in overlap and cut the wide ribbon to this length. Arrange the feathers in the centre of the ribbon on the reverse side. Cut a strip of felt the same width as the ribbon and glue it onto the feathers. This will help to secure them in place.

2 Sew a few lines of decorative stitching along the ribbon, using colourful embroidery threads. With the right sides facing, sew the two ends of the ribbon together.

3 To make each plait (braid), you will need approximately 45 equal strands of wool. Tie a piece of wool around one end of each bundle. Ask a friend to help you with the plaiting by holding one end of the bundle tight while you plait. Tie a piece of ribbon in a bow at the end of each plait.

4 Sew or glue the plaits onto the inside of the headdress, so that they lie either side of your face. For the face, use bright colours to paint three zig-zag lines on each cheek.

Prince

To make a sword, follow the instructions given for the knight's costume. The cloak was made from a piece of fabric found at a flea market and was decorated with a piece of tinsel to match the crown.

YOU WILL NEED
tape measure
pencil
scissors
cardboard
silver paint
paintbrush
coloured foil paper
glue
glitter
tinsel
fabric for cloak
safety pins

coloured foil paper

scissors

glitter

glue

tinsel

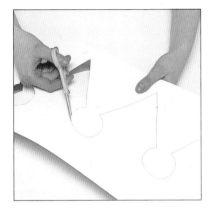

1 Measure around your head with a tape measure so that you know approximately how big to make the crown. Draw and cut out the crown from a piece of cardboard.

2 Paint the cardboard silver and leave the paint to dry thoroughly. Cut shapes out of coloured foil paper and glue them onto the crown. Paint dots of glue onto the shapes and sprinkle on some glitter.

3 Glue a piece of tinsel around the rim of the crown and leave the glue to dry.

4 Glue the two ends of the crown together to fit on your head and leave the glue to dry before you try the crown on. Pin the fabric to your shoulders to make a cloak.

Princess

If you have always dreamed of being a beautiful young princess, and imagined living in a castle, dress up in this costume and maybe your dream will come true.

YOU WILL NEED
tape measure
fabric for hat
fabric interfacing (optional)
pencil
scissors
needle and thread
chiffon fabric
wool
narrow ribbon
braid

thread

fabric interfacing

fabric

scissors

braid

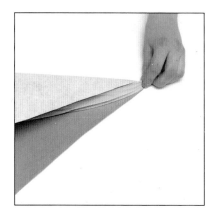

1 Measure the width of your head with a tape measure, so that you know how wide to make the rim of the hat. If the fabric you are using needs to be stiffened, iron a piece of interfacing onto the reverse side. Draw and cut out a triangle with a curved base, making sure the rim measures the width of your head, with an allowance for sewing together. Sew a hem around the rim of the triangle and, with the right sides facing, fold the triangle in half, trapping a piece of chiffon fabric at the point of the cone.

2 Sew the cone together and turn it right side out.

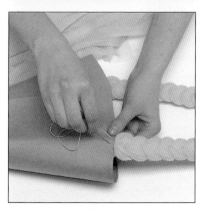

3 Following the instructions for the Native American, make a pair of woollen plaits (braids) and tie a piece of ribbon in a bow around the end of each one. Sew the plaits onto the inside of the hat, so that they lie either side of the face.

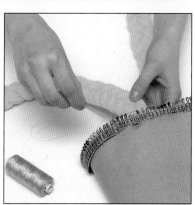

4 Sew a piece of braid around the rim of the hat, and arrange the chiffon fabric so that it trails down the side like a veil.

Hippy

Be loving and laid-back in this colourful flower-power costume. Search local flea markets and second-hand shops for bright clothes to wear with the accessories. Go completely wild and paint a flower on your cheek.

YOU WILL NEED
template for flower pendant
pencil
scissors
cardboard
newspaper
PVA (white) glue
bowl
water
paints
paintbrush
hole puncher
ribbon
fabric or old scarf
scraps of coloured felt
needle and thread
buttons
tissue and crepe paper
garden canes

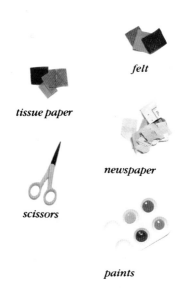

tissue paper

felt

newspaper

scissors

paints

buttons

1 Use the template to draw around and cut a piece of cardboard in the shape of a flower. Scrunch up small balls of newspaper and glue them in the centre of the flower.

2 Cover the flower in three layers of papier mâché as described in the introduction and leave to dry thoroughly in a warm place.

3 Paint the flower in lots of bright colours and leave to dry. Using a hole puncher, punch a hole in one of the petals and thread a piece of ribbon through.

4 For the headband you will need a band of bright fabric or an old scarf. Cut out different shaped flowers from coloured felt. Sew the flowers onto the headband and sew a button onto the centre of each flower.

5 To make a colourful bouquet of flowers, first cut out lots of shapes in tissue and crepe paper. Starting with the largest petal at the bottom, layer the petals on top of each other, piercing a hole through them with the garden cane.

6 Roll a piece of tissue paper with glue and place it in the centre of the flower on the stick. Fan out the petals to finish off.

NATURE FUN

Parts of a Tree

Trees are the giants of the plant world. See if you can find these different parts of a tree.

2 **Twigs:** In winter, twigs and branches can help you to identify a tree. From the top, these twigs are: birch, ash, apple, oak and willow.

3 **Trunk bark and roots:** We do not often see a tree's roots. These willow trees are growing by a pond. Can you see the fine, hairy rootlets?

1 **Leaves:** These come in many shapes and sizes. Some have toothed edges. Others are divided up into many smaller leaflets. Pine leaves are like needles.

4 **Flowers:** Some trees have flowers with petals. But many have green or yellow catkins and do not look like flowers at all.

6 **Cones:** Pines are usually evergreen. Most do not lose their leaves in winter. Their leaves are like needles. Their fruit are seeds which are carried in pine cones.

7 Deciduous trees like the walnut opposite lose their leaves in winter. Every autumn the green leaves change colour to yellow, brown or red. They shrivel and fall from the tree. Can you see them on the ground?

5 **Fruit:** There is a great variety of tree fruits and seeds. Fruit and nuts are spread by animals who try to eat them. Other seeds have wings that spin through the air like helicopters.

How Tall is a Tree?

Field guides and other books often tell us the height of a tree. But how do we actually measure it?

YOU WILL NEED
pencil
stick
tape measure or ruler
notebook

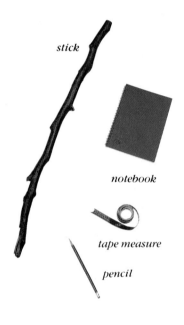

stick

notebook

tape measure

pencil

1 Stand in front of the tree. Hold out a pencil at arm's length so that you can see it and the tree at the same time. Ask a friend to stand at the bottom of the tree.

2 Line the pencil up so that the top of it is in line with the top of the tree. Move your thumb down the pencil until it is level with the bottom of the tree.

4 Mark the place where your friend is standing with a stick. Measure the distance from the stick to the tree. This distance is the same as the height of the tree. Record your findings in your notebook.

3 Turn the pencil so that it is horizontal, still keeping your thumb level with the bottom of the tree. Ask your friend to walk away from the trunk. Call and tell her to stop when she is level with the top of the pencil.

How Big and How Old is a Tree?

Some trees are very old. We can measure how big and old a tree is very easily.

YOU WILL NEED
rope
tape measure or ruler
notebook
pencil

notebook

rope

tape measure

pencil

1 How big is a tree? Take a piece of rope to measure the tree trunk. Put it around the tree and keep your finger on the place where the rope overlaps. A large oak tree like this one could be several hundred years old.

2 Lay the rope out straight on the ground and measure to the place you have marked with your finger. This will equal the distance around the outside of the trunk (the girth).

NATURE TIP

Next time you go for a walk look at the trees. How many really old trees can you find? These will be the tallest and/or those with the thickest trunks.

3 How old is a tree? The tree rings on a log can tell us its age. The tree grows a new ring every year.

4 Count the rings and you will discover the age of the log. If the tree has one hundred and fifty rings then the log is one hundred and fifty years old. Record your findings in your notebook with a pencil.

Growing a Tree

Trees are easy to grow at home. Collect some acorns, seeds or nuts in autumn and grow yourself a forest!

YOU WILL NEED
flowerpot
potting soil
acorn or other tree fruit such as nuts
   or seeds
plastic bag
rubber band
saucer
small trowel

flowerpot

potting soil

acorns

small trowel

plastic bag

rubber band

1 Fill the flowerpot with potting soil.

2 Push an acorn, nut or seed into the soil. Cover with more soil.

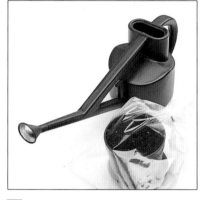

3 Water the flowerpot with just enough water to make the potting soil moist. Put the flowerpot into the plastic bag and seal the top with a rubber band. Leave on a windowsill until the acorn or seeds sprout. Be patient, this could take several weeks or even months.

4 Once the seeds have sprouted, remove the flowerpot from the plastic bag. Stand it in a saucer to catch any water that drains from the bottom. Keep the seedling on a windowsill and remember to water it regularly.

5 As your tree grows you will eventually need to repot it into a larger flowerpot.

6 When the young tree (or sapling) is 50–100 cm (18–39 in) tall, plant it outside in a place where it can grow into a large tree.

7 Look at the picture on the right. Can you see three stages in the life of an oak tree? The children are holding a seedling and a young sapling. Behind them is a young oak tree. Eventually this small tree will grow into an old giant of a tree – just like the one that was measured earlier.

Keeping Caterpillars

This is a nice clean way to keep caterpillars. Eventually they will turn into pupae and then into beautiful butterflies and moths.

YOU WILL NEED
collecting pot
plastic bottle
scissors
paper towels
large jar
sticky tape
gauze or netting
rubber band or string

plastic bottle

collecting pot

scissors

gauze

sticky tape

rubber band

1 Look for some caterpillars living on cabbages and other plants. Put them in a collecting pot. At the same time, collect some leaves from the plants that you found the caterpillars living on.

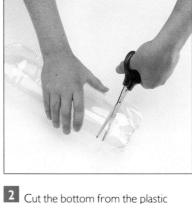

2 Cut the bottom from the plastic bottle with a pair of scissors.

3 Take a bunch of leaves and foliage that you found the caterpillars on. Wrap a piece of paper towel around the stalks of the leaves.

4 Put the leaves inside the bottle and push the stalks through the neck so that the tissue forms a plug.

5 Stand the bottle neck-down in a jar of water. Make sure that the plant stalks are standing in the water. Tape the bottle to the jar if it is wobbly and does not stand firmly.

NATURE TIP

Every few days, clean out the bottle, wash it, dry it, and give the caterpillars fresh plants to eat. Eventually the caterpillars will pupate. They will turn into sausage-shaped pupae. You can keep them until the butterflies or moths emerge, and then you must release them outside.

6 Put the caterpillars inside the bottle. Cover the top with a piece of gauze. Hold it in place with a rubber band or tie with string. Feed your caterpillars regularly.

Plaster Casts

Animals often leave their footprints in soft mud and sand. Make plaster casts of them to keep a permanent record. You can paint them when the plaster is dry.

YOU WILL NEED
strip of card (cardboard)
paperclip
plaster of Paris
water
bucket or plastic tub
spoon
small trowel
old brush or toothbrush (optional)

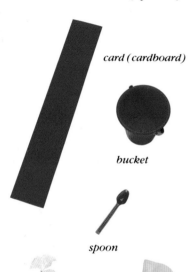

card (cardboard)

bucket

spoon

plaster of Paris

water

paperclips

1 Look for animal footprints in mud and sand.

2 Select the clearest footprint.

3 Put the card (cardboard) around the print and secure with a paperclip. Push the card down slightly into the mud.

4 Next, mix the plaster of Paris. Put a small amount of water into the bucket. Add plaster powder and stir well.

5 Pour the plaster into the mould and leave to set.

6 Once set, use a small trowel to dig up the plaster and print. Clean off the soil and sand. You may need to use an old brush or toothbrush to clean into all the small cracks.

Keeping Slugs and Snails

Slugs and snails can be kept in a tank. Here, you can learn how to make them a comfortable home.

You WILL NEED
gravel
small tank or large plastic
   ice cream container
soil
moss and grass
small stones, pieces of bark and
   dried leaves
gauze or netting
string
scissors

small tank
gauze
string

soil
gravel
moss
stone, bark and dried leaves

1 Put a layer of gravel in the bottom of the tank or container.

2 Cover the gravel with a layer of soil.

NATURE TIP

Keep your snails in a cool place. Feed them on a small amount of breakfast cereal (not too sugary), and small pieces of fruit and vegetables. Add fresh grass and leaves when needed.

3 Plant pieces of moss and grass in the soil. Add stones, bark and the dried leaves. Water the tank just enough to moisten the soil.

4 Put in a few slugs or snails and cover the tank with a piece of gauze or netting. Tie it down with string or replace the lid. Make sure that it has plenty of air holes.

Feeding Winter Birds

Choose some of these ideas to feed birds in winter.

YOU WILL NEED

Choose food from the following:
dried bird food
dried seed heads such as corn cobs,
    millet and sunflower
peanuts
bread and cake crumbs
coconut
lard or other hard fat
chopped bacon rind

bowl of water
peanut feeder
string
scissors
spoon
supermarket packaging such as plastic
    pots or nets

peanut feeder

lard

plastic pot

chopped rind

dried bird food

corn cob

bread

peanuts

string

1 Dried food is the easiest to put out. Give the birds grain, sunflower seeds, peanuts (but not in spring), bread and cake crumbs. Do not forget to also give them a bowl of water to drink.

2 Hanging food allows birds to perch on the food. Hang strings of peanuts, half a coconut, a dried sweet corn cob, millet or other seed heads from the screw-eyes on your bird feeder. You can also hang these foods from the branches of nearby trees. Put loose peanuts in a peanut feeder, if feeding in the winter.

3 Birdy cake is a rich food for cold winter weather. Soften lard or a similar hard fat in a warm place. Mash in mixed grains, crumbs, bread, chopped bacon and rinds. Mix well.

4 Press into supermarket packaging such as plastic pots and nets. Set until hard in a refrigerator. When set, tip the birdy cake from the pots and put on a bird table or hang the nets beneath it.

Pond and River Dipping

Beneath the surface of the water lives a rich and
varied animal and plant life. Dip into the world of a
pond or river using a fishing or plankton net and
discover the creatures that live there.

YOU WILL NEED
ice cream container or bucket
fishing and/or plankton net
shallow white dishes, made by cutting
   the top from an ice cream container
paintbrush
jam jar or tank
notebook
pencil

net

jam jar

pencil

notebook

ice cream container

paintbrush

1 Fill an ice cream container or bucket
with pond water. You will then have
something to put your animals in as soon
as you catch them.

2 Sweep the fishing or plankton net
through the weeds.

3 Pour the water from the plankton
net into an ice cream container or bucket
by pushing the jar up through the net. Pull
the net back and pour the water out.

4 You will soon catch many different
animals. Here are two types of pond snail
– a round Ramshorn Snail and a pointed
Greater Pond Snail.

5 Carefully pick out the animals you
have just caught with a paintbrush and
place them into a clean shallow dish or
ice cream container, of water. You will
have caught a lot of rubbish such as dead
leaves, and the clean water will help you
see the animals more clearly.

!SAFETY TIP

Take care around water, no matter how shallow it seems.

6 You can also put them into a large jam jar, or small tank. Identify the species you have found and make notes in your notebook. Visit different ponds, lakes, and rivers. Do you find the same species living in different places?

Making a Freshwater Aquarium

Pond animals can be kept easily in an aquarium. Watch the busy lives of your pond animals.

YOU WILL NEED
aquarium gravel
bucket
large tank
newspaper
waterplants
stones or rocks
seashells (optional)
fish or other creatures collected from
a pond or river

rock

aquarium gravel

newspaper

tank

1 Wash the gravel in a bucket. Keep stirring it under running water. You must do this thoroughly to remove dirt from the stones which will make the water in your tank cloudy.

2 Put the gravel in the bottom of the tank. Once you have filled the tank with water it will be too heavy to move – so decide where you want to keep it now. Do not place the tank in bright sunshine or the water will get too hot and your animals will die.

3 Put the newspaper over the top of the gravel. Slowly pour the water on to of the paper. This prevents the water from becoming too cloudy.

4 The water will be slightly cloudy, so leave the tank to clear for several days.

5 Add some waterplants and the rocks. Put the roots of the plants under the rocks to stop them from floating up to the surface. If you use any seashells, make sure that they have been well washed in fresh water to remove any salt that they may contain.

6 Put in the animals that you have collected from a pond or river. If you are going to have fish in the aquarium, only choose small ones or else they will eat all of your pond animals.

Beachcombing at the Seaside

We all like to go to the seaside. Be a nature detective on the beach and see what treasures you can find.

YOU WILL NEED
bucket
plastic bags
notebook
pencil

pencil

notebook

plastic bags

bucket

1 Look for animals under seaweed and rocks where they stay nice and damp. Cuttlefish, crab and urchin shells, feathers and other animals are often washed up. You will find them at the highest place reached by the tide, known as the strandline.

2 You will find a variety of shells all over the beach.

3 Look for unusual stones and pebble sculptures, fossils and minerals. The holes in this large stone were drilled by rock-boring clams. Can you see the Indian's head? This is a real stone that was just picked up on a beach.

4 Who lives under the sand? Look for worm holes and dig down to find the worm beneath. Collect animals and shells and put them in a bucket or plastic bags. Make notes in your notebook, and release living creatures afterwards.

! 5 A lot of garbage is washed up onto the beach. Ropes, plastic and driftwood are harmless, but fishing tackle, bottles and canisters can be dangerous. Take care and do not touch. Some can contain dangerous chemicals.

Rock Pools

Many animals such as shrimps, crabs and baby fish live in rock pools. Here they find a safe place to wait until the tide comes in again.

YOU WILL NEED
fishing net
bucket
plastic bags
notebook
pencil

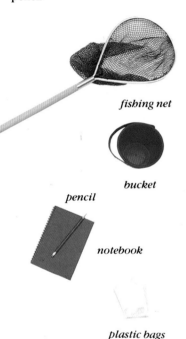

fishing net

bucket

pencil

notebook

plastic bags

! SAFETY TIP
Take care on slippery rocks. Do not get cut off by incoming tides.

1 When the tide goes out, animals on the beach must close up or hide and wait until the water returns. In the rock pool however, the animals can continue to swim and feed.

2 Some animals such as limpets and anemones attach themselves to rocks. They can move, but only very slowly.

3 Sweep a fishing net through the sandy bottom of the pool. You may catch shrimps, crabs and tiny fish that lie buried in the sand.

! 4 Be careful if you find a crab. Do not handle it roughly because you may damage its legs. You can pick it up safely by holding it across the back of its shell. This way it cannot nip you!

5 Lift up rocks carefully. Many animals live underneath them. Always replace rocks gently so that you do not damage the microhabitat and the animals underneath.

6 Collect animals in a bucket or plastic bag. Identify them and make notes in your notebook. In this bucket there are hermit crabs, shore crabs, periwinkles and a sea anemone. Do not forget to release them into the water afterwards.

Potpourri

Potpourri has been used for centuries to make rooms and stored linen smell nice and fresh.

YOU WILL NEED
fresh flowers
fresh herbs, such as lavender and
  rosemary
scissors
string
foil dish or tray
bowl
spices, such as nutmeg, cinnamon
  sticks and cloves (optional)
airtight jars or bags

lavender

fresh flowers

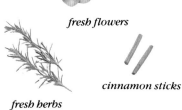

cinnamon sticks

fresh herbs

foil dish

string

scissors

1 Pick the flowers and herbs. This plant is lavender.

2 Cut the herbs and tie them into bunches. This plant is rosemary.

3 Hang the bunches of herbs up in a warm place to dry.

4 Put fresh rose petals, small flowers, flower buds, herb leaves and herb flowers onto a foil dish or tray. Put them somewhere warm such as an airing cupboard or near a radiator to dry.

5 When the herbs and flowers are completely dry, strip the leaves from the herb bunches. Put them into a bowl with the dried petals and flowerheads.

6 Add the spices (if using) and mix well. If you wish, you can also add a few drops of perfumed oil. Mix well. Store in airtight jars or bags. To use, place in a shallow dish or basket so that the scent of the flowers, herbs and spices can escape into the air.

Make your own Garden

Create your own indoor garden paradise within a
cardboard box. If you use moss from the garden you
may need to replace it after a few days if it dries out.

YOU WILL NEED
scissors
ruler
cardboard box
brown paint
paintbrush
small mirror
magazine pictures
bits and pieces from the garden such
 as moss, earth, gravel, ivy and twigs
shells
plasticine

shells

leaves

gravel

moss

ivy

plasticine

mirror

magazine picture

1 With a pair of scissors, cut the cardboard box so that it is just 4 cm (1 ½ in) deep and paint it brown. Allow to dry.

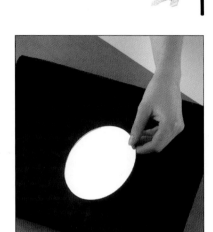

2 For the pond, place the mirror in the bottom of the box.

3 For the garden, arrange the magazine pictures, moss and shells inside the box.

4 For the trees, stick the twigs into a piece of plasticine and place them among the moss and shells.

5 Scatter the gravel and earth to cover any bare patches.

6 Finish off the garden by decorating it with pieces of ivy.

Making a Terrarium

Ferns grow in damp places among rocks and in woodlands. You can make yourself an indoor garden by growing them in a large jar or bottle.

YOU WILL NEED
gravel
large plastic jar or bottle with lid or
    stopper
charcoal
potting soil
spoon taped to a long stick
ferns and other plants

plastic jar

plants

spoon taped to a stick

gravel

charcoal

potting soil

1 Put a layer of gravel in the bottom of the jar or bottle.

2 Put a layer of charcoal on top.

3 Put in a layer of potting soil. Smooth and level the soil with the long-handled spoon.

4 Again using the long-handled spoon, plant the ferns and other plants.

5 Gently add enough water to moisten the soil.

6 Replace the lid or stopper on the jar or bottle. The moisture is kept inside the jar so the plants rarely need watering.

Growing Curly Beans

Here is a simple plant experiment that you can easily do at home.

YOU WILL NEED
paper towels
jam jar
bean or pea seeds such as French (string), runner or mung beans

paper towels

jam jar

bean seeds

NATURE TIP

Bean shoots will always try to grow upwards and towards the light. Look at the large picture on this page. The beans top left are normal beans, growing straight up. The other two jars contain curly beans.

1 Fold a piece of paper towel in half, roll it up and put inside the jam jar.

2 Put several bean seeds between the paper and the side of the jam jar. Pour water into the bottom of the jam jar to a depth of approximately 2 cm (¾ in).

3 When the beans have sprouted a long shoot, turn the jam jar on its side.

4 Put the jam jar on a windowsill and turn the shoot away from the light. Keep turning the jam jar so that the shoot is turned away from the light. You will soon grow curly beans.

Colouring Celery and Flowers

This experiment works almost like magic! You can change white flowers and celery to almost any colour you like.

YOU WILL NEED
jam jar
brightly coloured water-soluble ink or dye
stalk of celery with leaves
white flowers such as carnations, chrysanthemums or daisies

water-soluble ink

celery

flowers

jam jar

1 Half-fill the jam jar with water.

2 Add some ink or dye.

!NATURE TIP

If you have difficulty making this experiment work, try again with another type or colour of dye. Remember, you will not be able to eat the celery once it has been dyed!

3 Stand some celery or flowers in the dye or ink solution.

4 You can make celery or flowers that are half one colour and half another. Split the celery or flower stalk lengthwise and put half in a jam jar of one coloured dye and the other half-stalk in the second jar containing a different colour.

Growing a Pineapple

We all see pineapple in the supermarket. Did you know that you can often use one to grow your own pineapple plant?

YOU WILL NEED
flowerpot
potting soil
fresh pineapple
plastic bag

flowerpot

plastic bag

potting soil

pineapple

1 Fill the flowerpot with potting soil.

2 Twist the top from the pineapple. (You may need an adult to help you with this.)

3 Remove the lower leaves from the stalk. Plant the stalk in the potting soil.

4 Water and place the flowerpot in a plastic bag. Leave in a warm sunny place. Remove the bag when the roots have started to grow. Water your pineapple regularly. Some may eventually produce fruit if kept in a warm greenhouse. Most just make nice houseplants.

Growing Exotic Plants from Seed

Other exotic plants can be grown from the seeds and pips that we find inside fruit.

YOU WILL NEED
fresh fruit
sieve
knife
paper towel
flowerpot
potting soil
plastic bag

paper towel

knife

flowerpot

plastic bag

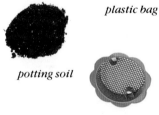

potting soil

sieve

fresh fruit

! **1** Eat the fruit but save the seeds. Wash the seeds in the sieve. Ask an adult to help you to remove any flesh with a sharp knife. Dry the seeds on a piece of paper towel.

2 Fill the flowerpot with potting soil. Plant the seeds in the soil. Cover them with more potting soil.

3 Water, and put the flowerpot in a plastic bag. Keep in a warm place. Some seeds will sprout quickly, others may take longer. Remove the bag when the sprouts first appear. Keep the flowerpot on a windowsill. Transplant into larger flowerpots as the plants grow larger. The plants in the picture above were grown from supermarket fruit. On the left is a lemon, and on the right a tree tomato.

Autumn Leaves

Every autumn deciduous trees lose their leaves. A tiny layer of cells grow across each leaf stalk like a wall, and the leaf shrivels, dies and falls off. As the leaf dies, it changes colour to yellow, brown, orange, red or purple. Collect fallen leaves and make a collage with them.

YOU WILL NEED
autumn leaves
newspaper
book
large envelope
PVA (white) glue
card (cardboard) or paper

newspaper

book   *PVA (white) glue*

large envelope

card (cardboard)

autumn leaves

1 Collect as many different autumn leaves as you can.

2 Place the leaves between the folds of a newspaper. Lightly press them by putting a book on top.

3 You can store the flat leaves in an envelope until you need them.

4 Glue the leaves onto a piece of card (cardboard).

5 Make a collection of different types of leaf or use them to make a collage, picture or to decorate greetings cards.

COOKERY FUN

Most dishes need something to go with them, to turn them into a complete meal.
Here are some quick and easy ideas for accompaniments.

Making Mashed Potatoes

Check the labelling on the packets to see which potatoes are good for mashing: or ask your greengrocer.

Serves 4

INGREDIENTS
450 g/1 lb potatoes, peeled and
    quartered
25 g/1 oz/2 tbsp butter
30 ml/2 tbsp milk or cream
salt and pepper

1 Cook the potatoes in a pan with enough room to mash them. Cover with water, add a little salt and bring the water to the boil. Turn down the heat and simmer for 20–25 minutes. The potatoes should feel tender and fall off a sharp knife when cooked.

COOK'S TIP
Add two crushed cloves of garlic or a handful of chopped fresh herbs, to make a real change.

2 Drain them in a colander and return them to the pan. Add the butter, milk or cream and black pepper and use a potato masher to squash the potatoes and flatten all the lumps. Add more milk if you like them really soft.

Cooking Rice

Measure rice in a jug, by volume rather than by weight, for best results.

Serves 2

INGREDIENTS
10 ml/2 tsp oil
150 ml/¼ pint/⅔ cup long grain
    white rice
300 ml/½ pint/1¼ cups boiling water
    or stock
salt

COOK'S TIP
Some types of easy-cook rice may not take as long; check cooking times on the packet.

1 Heat the oil in a saucepan and add the rice. Stir to coat all the grains with the oil.

2 Pour on the boiling water or stock, add a little salt and stir once, before putting on the lid. Turn down the heat so the liquid is just simmering gently and walk away. Leave it alone for 15 minutes.

3 Lift the lid carefully (away from you) and check whether the rice is tender and that the liquid has almost gone. Fluff up the grains of rice with a fork and serve immediately.

Cooking Pasta

Pasta comes in lots of different shapes, sizes and colours. Green pasta has spinach in it, red pasta has tomato, and brown pasta is made from wholewheat flour. Egg pasta has extra eggs in the dough. Allow about 115 g/4 oz dried pasta per person if it is the main ingredient, and a little less if it is to accompany a meal, although this may vary according to how hungry you are!

Serves 4

INGREDIENTS
350–450 g/12 oz–1 lb dried pasta
salt

COOK'S TIP
Fresh pasta is also available, but its cooking times are shorter – check pack instructions.

1 Bring a large saucepan of water to boil. Add a little salt. Add the pasta to the pan, a little at a time so that the water stays at a rolling boil.

2 Cook for 8–12 minutes, depending on what type of pasta you are using – spaghetti will not take as long as the thicker penne pasta. It should be "al dente" when cooked, which means it still has some firmness to it and isn't completely soft and soggy.

3 Drain the pasta well in a colander and tip it back into the pan. Pour a sauce over or toss in a little melted butter.

Making Salad Dressing

Green or mixed salads add crunch and freshness to heavy meaty meals like lasagne or barbecued ribs, but they are bland and boring without a dressing like this one.

Serves 4

INGREDIENTS
15 ml/1 tbsp white wine vinegar
10 ml/2 tsp coarse-grain mustard
salt
freshly ground black pepper
30 ml/2 tbsp oil

COOK'S TIP
Mix 30 ml/2 tbsp oil with 15 ml/1 tbsp lemon juice, for a tangier dressing. Add chopped fresh herbs for extra flavour.

1 Put the vinegar and mustard in a bowl or jug. Whisk well, then add a little salt and pepper.

2 Add the oil slowly, about 5 ml/1 tsp at a time, whisking constantly. Pour the dressing over the salad just before serving so that the lettuce stays crisp. Use two spoons to toss the salad and coat it with the dressing.

Skinny Dips

Potato skins in disguise, with a delicious spicy dip.

Serves 4

INGREDIENTS
8 large potatoes, scrubbed
30–45 ml/2–3 tbsp oil
90 ml/6 tbsp mayonnaise
30 ml/2 tbsp natural (plain) yogurt
5 ml/1 tsp curry paste
15 ml/1 tbsp roughly chopped fresh
   coriander (cilantro)
salt

curry paste

potatoes

mayonnaise

fresh coriander
(cilantro)

natural (plain) yogurt

1 Preheat the oven to 190°C/375°F/
Gas Mark 5. Arrange the potatoes in a
roasting tin (pan), prick them all over with
a fork and cook for 45 minutes, or until
tender. Leave to cool slightly.

2 Carefully cut each potato into
quarters lengthways, holding it with a
clean dish towel if it's still a bit hot.

3 Scoop out some of the centre with a
knife or spoon and put the skins back in
the roasting tin. Save the cooked potato
for making fish cakes.

4 Brush the skins with oil and sprinkle
with salt before putting them back in the
oven. Cook for 30–40 minutes more,
until they are crisp and brown, brushing
them occasionally with more oil.

5 Meanwhile, put the mayonnaise,
yogurt, curry paste and coriander
(cilantro) in a small bowl and mix together
well. Leave for 30–40 minutes for the
flavour to develop.

6 Put the dip in a clean bowl and
arrange the skins around the edge.
Serve hot, sprinkled with the remaining
coriander (cilantro).

COOK'S TIP

If there is just one of you, prick one
large potato all over with a fork and
microwave on HIGH for 6–8 minutes,
until tender. Scoop out the centre,
brush with oil and grill (broil) till
brown.

See-in-the-Dark Soup

Stop stumbling around when the lights are off – eat more carrots! Serve with crunchy toast.

Serves 4

INGREDIENTS
15 ml/1 tbsp oil
1 onion, sliced
450 g/1 lb carrots, sliced
75 g/3 oz/½ cup split red lentils
1.2 litres/2 pints/5 cups vegetable
  stock
5 ml/1 tsp ground coriander
  (cilantro)
75 ml/3 tbsp chopped fresh parsley
salt and pepper

vegetable stock

onion

parsley

red lentils

carrots

coriander (cilantro)

1 Heat the oil and fry the onion until it is starting to brown. Add the sliced carrots and fry gently for 4–5 minutes, stirring them often, until they soften.

3 Turn down the heat, put the lid on and leave to simmer gently for 30 minutes, or until the lentils are cooked.

COOK'S TIP
Push the soup through a sieve with a wooden spoon or leave it chunky, if you don't have a food processor or blender.

2 Meanwhile, put the lentils in a small bowl and cover with cold water. Pour off any bits that float. Tip the lentils into a sieve and rinse under cold running water.

4 Add the lentils, stock and coriander (cilantro) to the saucepan with salt and pepper. Bring the soup to the boil.

5 Add the chopped parsley and cook for 5 minutes more. Remove from the heat and allow to cool slightly.

6 Carefully put the soup into a food processor or blender and whizz until it is smooth. (You may have to do this a half at a time.) Rinse the saucepan before pouring the soup back in and add a little water if it looks too thick. Heat up again before serving.

Nutty Chicken Kebabs

A tasty Thai starter that's quick to make and uses everyone's favourite spread in the dip.

Serves 4

INGREDIENTS
30 ml/2 tbsp oil
15 ml/1 tbsp lemon juice
450 g/1 lb boneless, skinless chicken
   breasts, cut in small cubes

FOR THE DIP
5 ml/1 tsp chilli powder
75 ml/5 tbsp water
15 ml/1 tbsp oil
1 small onion, grated
1 garlic clove, peeled and crushed
30 ml/2 tbsp lemon juice
60 ml/4 tbsp crunchy peanut butter
5 ml/1 tsp salt
5 ml/1 tsp ground coriander
   (cilantro)
sliced cucumber and lemon wedges,
   to serve

lemon
juice

crunchy
peanut
butter

onion

oil

chilli powder

chicken breast

ground
coriander
(cilantro)

garlic

1 Soak 12 wooden skewers in water, to prevent them from burning during grilling. Mix the oil and lemon juice together in a bowl and stir in the cubed chicken. Cover and leave to marinate for at least 30 minutes.

2 Thread four or five cubes on each wooden skewer. Cook under a hot grill (broiler), turning often, until cooked and browned, about 10 minutes. Cut one piece open to check it is cooked right through; this is very important, especially for chicken.

3 Meanwhile make the dip. Mix the chilli powder with 15 ml/1 tbsp water. Heat the oil in a small frying pan and fry the onion and garlic until tender.

4 Turn down the heat and add the chilli paste and the remaining ingredients and stir well. Stir in more water if the sauce is too thick and put it into a small bowl. Serve warm, with the chicken kebabs, cucumber slices and lemon wedges.

Eggs in a Blanket

A hearty brunch or lunch to tuck into on a chilly day, with chunks of wholewheat bread.

Serves 4

INGREDIENTS
1 aubergine (eggplant), sliced
5 ml/1 tsp salt
15 ml/1 tbsp oil
1 onion, sliced
1 garlic clove, peeled and crushed
1 yellow bell pepper, seeded and
    sliced
1 courgette (zucchini), sliced
400 g/14 oz can chopped tomatoes
120 ml/4 fl oz/½ cup water
10 ml/2 tsp dried mixed herbs
4 eggs

aubergine (eggplant)

pepper

courgette (zucchini)

salt

chopped tomatoes

eggs

onion

garlic

mixed herbs

1 Arrange the aubergine (eggplant) slices on a plate, sprinkle with salt and leave for 30 minutes. Rinse and squeeze out as much juice as you can.

2 Heat the oil in a large frying pan. Fry the onion until it starts to soften. Add the garlic, pepper, courgette (zucchini) and aubergine and fry for 3–4 minutes.

3 Add the chopped tomatoes, water and herbs. Stir in salt and pepper to taste. Simmer gently for 5 minutes.

4 Make four shallow dips in the mixture and break an egg into each one. Cover the pan with a lid or foil and simmer for 8–12 minutes, until the eggs are set and the vegetables are tender.

Bacon Twists

Making bread is always fun, so try this tasty version and add that extra twist to your breakfast. Serve with soft cheese with herbs.

Makes 12

INGREDIENTS
450 g/1 lb/4 cups strong white flour
6 g/¼ oz sachet easy-blend yeast
2.5 ml/½ tsp salt
400 ml/14 fl oz/1¾ cups hand-hot
 water
12 bacon rashers (strips)
1 egg, beaten

water
flour
egg
yeast
salt
bacon

1 Mix the flour, yeast and salt in a bowl and stir them together. Add a little of the water and mix with a knife. Add the remaining water and use your hands to pull the mixture together, to make a sticky dough.

2 Turn the dough on to a lightly floured surface and knead it for 5 minutes, or until the dough is smooth and stretchy.

3 Divide into 12 pieces and roll each one into a sausage shape.

4 Lay each bacon rasher (strip) on a chopping board and run the back of the knife down its length, to stretch it slightly. Wind a rasher of bacon round each dough "sausage".

5 Brush the "sausages" with beaten egg and arrange them on a lightly oiled baking sheet. Leave somewhere warm for 30 minutes, or until they have doubled in size. Preheat the oven to 200°C/400°F/Gas 6 and cook the "sausages" for 20–25 minutes, until cooked and browned.

COOK'S TIP
This same basic dough mix can be used to make rolls or a loaf of bread. Tap the base of the breadstick – if it sounds hollow, it's cooked.

Give 'em a Roasting

Don't stick to roast potatoes! A good roasting brings out the colours and flavours of other vegetables too.

Serves 4

INGREDIENTS

1 aubergine (eggplant), cut in large
   chunks
15 ml/1 tbsp salt
1 red bell pepper, seeded and cut in
   thick strips
1 green bell pepper, seeded and cut in
   thick strips
1 yellow bell pepper, seeded and cut
   in thick strips
1 courgette (zucchini), cut in large
   chunks
1 onion, cut in thick slices
115 g/4 oz small mushrooms
225 g/8 oz plum tomatoes, quartered
75 ml/5 tbsp olive oil
4–5 thyme sprigs
2 oregano sprigs
3–4 rosemary sprigs
sea salt and freshly ground black
   pepper

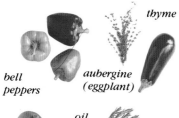

bell peppers   aubergine (eggplant)   thyme

oil   onion   rosemary

courgette (zucchini)   plum tomatoes

mushrooms   oregano

1 Arrange the aubergine (eggplant) chunks on a plate and sprinkle them with the salt. Leave for 30 minutes.

2 Squeeze the aubergine to remove as much liquid as possible. Rinse off the salt. This process stops the aubergine tasting so bitter.

3 Preheat the oven to 200°C/400°F/ Gas 6. Arrange all the vegetables, including the aubergine, in a roasting tin (pan) and drizzle the oil over.

4 Scatter most of the herb sprigs in among the vegetables and season well. Put the tin into the hot oven and cook for 20–25 minutes.

5 Turn the vegetables over and cook them for 15 minutes more, or until they are tender and browned.

6 Scatter the remaining fresh herb sprigs over the cooked vegetables just before serving.

Wicked Tortilla Wedges

A tortilla is a thick omelette with lots of cooked potatoes in it. It is very popular in Spain, where it is cut in thick slices like a cake and served with bread. Try it with sliced tomato salad.

Serves 4

INGREDIENTS
30 ml/2 tbsp oil
675 g/1½ lb potatoes, cut in small
    chunks
1 onion, sliced
115 g/4 oz mushrooms, sliced
115 g/4 oz/1 cup frozen peas, thawed
50 g/2 oz/⅓ cup frozen corn kernels,
    thawed
4 eggs
150 ml/¼ pint/⅔ cup milk
10 ml/2 tsp Cajun seasoning
30 ml/2 tbsp chopped fresh parsley
salt and pepper

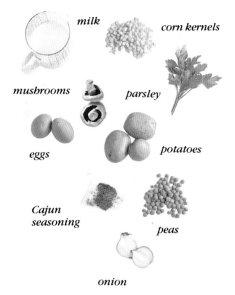

milk   *corn kernels*

mushrooms   *parsley*

eggs   *potatoes*

Cajun seasoning   *peas*

onion

1 Heat the oil in a large frying pan and fry the potatoes and onion for 3–4 minutes, stirring often. Turn down the heat, cover the pan and fry gently for another 8–10 minutes, until the potatoes are almost tender.

2 Add the mushrooms to the pan and cook for 2–3 minutes more, stirring often, until they have softened.

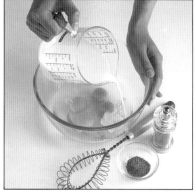

4 Put the eggs, milk and Cajun seasoning in a bowl. Add salt and pepper to taste and beat well.

3 Add the peas and corn and stir them into the potato mixture.

5 Level the top of the vegetables and scatter the parsley on top. Pour the egg mixture over and cook over a low heat for 10–15 minutes.

6 Put the pan under a hot grill (broiler) to set the top of the tortilla. Serve hot or cold, cut into wedges.

COOK'S TIP

Use less Cajun seasoning if you don't like spicy food. Make sure the frying pan can be used under the grill (broiler).

Homeburgers

These look the same as ordinary burgers, but watch out for the soft cheese centre. Serve with chips (fries) and sliced tomatoes.

Serves 4

INGREDIENTS
450 g/1 lb lean minced (ground) beef
2 slices of bread, crusts removed
1 egg
4 spring onions (scallions), roughly
    chopped
1 garlic clove, peeled and chopped
15 ml/1 tbsp mango chutney
10 ml/2 tsp dried mixed herbs
50 g/2 oz/⅓ cup mozzarella cheese
salt and pepper
4 burger buns, to serve

1 Put the mince, bread, egg, spring onions (scallions) and garlic in a food processor. Add a little salt and pepper and whizz until evenly blended. Add the chutney and herbs and whizz again.

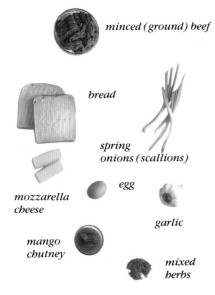

minced (ground) beef
bread
spring onions (scallions)
mozzarella cheese
egg
garlic
mango chutney
mixed herbs

2 Divide the mixture into four equal portions and pat flat, with damp hands, to stop the meat from sticking.

3 Cut the cheese into four equal pieces and put one in the centre of each piece of beef. Wrap the meat round the cheese to make a fat burger. Chill for 30 minutes. Preheat the grill (broiler).

4 Put the burgers on a rack under the hot grill, but not too close or they will burn on the outside before the middle has cooked properly. Cook them for 5–8 minutes on each side then put each burger in a roll, with your favourite trimmings.

Popeye's Pie

Tuck into this layered pie and you, too, can have bulging muscles!

Serves 4

INGREDIENTS

75 g/3 oz/⅓ cup butter
5 ml/1 tsp grated nutmeg
900 g/2 lb fresh spinach, washed and large stalks removed
115 g/4 oz/⅔ cup feta cheese, crumbled
50 g/2 oz Cheddar cheese, grated
275 g/10 oz filo pastry sheets
10 ml/2 tsp mixed ground cinnamon, nutmeg and black pepper

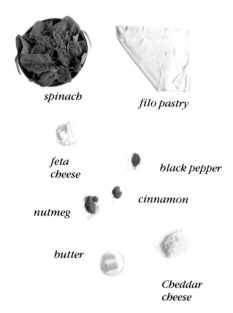

spinach

filo pastry

feta
cheese

black pepper

nutmeg

cinnamon

butter

Cheddar
cheese

1 Melt 25 g/1 oz/2 tbsp of the butter in a large frying pan, add the nutmeg and the spinach and season well. Cover and cook for 5 minutes, or until the spinach is tender. Drain well, pressing out as much liquid as possible.

2 Preheat the oven to 160°C/325°F/Gas 3. Melt the remaining butter in a small saucepan. Mix the cheeses together in a bowl and season them with salt and pepper. Unfold the pastry so the sheets are flat. Use one to line part of the base of a small, deep-sided, greased roasting tin (pan). Brush with melted butter. Keep the remaining filo sheets covered with a damp dish towel: they dry out very quickly.

3 Continue to lay pastry sheets across the base and up the sides of the tin, brushing each time with butter, until two-thirds of the pastry has been used. Don't worry if they flop over the top edges – they will be tidied up later.

4 Mix together the grated cheeses and spinach and spread them into the tin. Fold the pastry edges over. Crumple up the remaining sheets of pastry and arrange them over the top of the filling. Brush with melted butter and sprinkle the mixed spices over the top. Cook the pie for 45 minutes. Raise the oven temperature to 200°C/400°F/Gas 6, for 10–15 minutes more, to brown the top. Serve hot or cold.

Sticky Fingers

You have to like messy food to eat this popular dish, so plenty of napkins please! Juicy tomatoes make a refreshing accompaniment.

Serves 4

INGREDIENTS
30 ml/2 tbsp oil
1 onion, chopped
1 garlic clove, crushed
30 ml/2 tbsp tomato purée
15 ml/1 tbsp white wine vinegar
45 ml/3 tbsp clear honey
5 ml/1 tsp dried mixed herbs
2.5 ml/½ tsp chilli powder
150 ml/¼ pint/⅔ cup chicken stock
8 chicken thighs
375 g/12 oz spare ribs

FOR THE POTATOES
675 g/1½ lb potatoes, cubed
30 ml/2 tbsp oil
1 large onion, sliced
1 garlic clove, crushed
salt and pepper

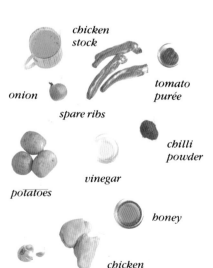

chicken stock

onion

spare ribs

tomato purée

chilli powder

vinegar

potatoes

honey

chicken

garlic

mixed herbs

1 Heat the oil in a saucepan and fry the onion and garlic until the onion starts to soften.

2 Add the tomato purée, vinegar, honey, herbs, chilli powder and stock and bring to the boil. Lower the heat and simmer for 15–20 minutes, when the sauce should have thickened.

3 Preheat the oven to 190°C/375°F/Gas 5. Arrange the chicken and ribs in a roasting tin (pan).

4 Spoon the sauce evenly over the meat and cook for 30 minutes. Turn the meat over to ensure that it is coated evenly in the sauce.

5 Cook for 45 minutes more, turning the meat several times and spooning the sauce over. The meat should be really browned and sticky.

6 Meanwhile, put the potatoes in lightly salted water, bring to the boil, then drain well. Heat the oil in a large frying pan. Fry the onion until it starts to turn brown. Add the potatoes and garlic and fry for 25–30 minutes, until everything is cooked through, browned and crisp.

Something Very Fishy

If you like getting your hands messy, this is the recipe for you! Serve with green vegetables and new potatoes.

Serves 4

INGREDIENTS
450 g/1 lb old potatoes, cut in small chunks
25 g/1 oz/2 tbsp butter or margarine
15 ml/1 tbsp milk
412 g/14½ oz can pink salmon, drained with skin and bones removed
1 egg, beaten
60 ml/4 tbsp plain flour
2 spring onions (scallions), finely chopped
4 sun-dried tomatoes in oil, chopped
grated rind of 1 lemon
25 g/1 oz sesame seeds

1 Cook the potatoes in boiling lightly salted water until tender. Drain and return to the saucepan. Add the butter or margarine and milk and mash until smooth. Season well.

2 Put the mashed potato in a bowl and beat in the salmon. Add the egg, flour, spring onions (scallions), tomatoes and lemon rind. Mix well.

3 Divide the mixture into 8 equal pieces and pat them into fish cake shapes, using floured hands.

salmon

butter

potatoes

milk

egg

flour

spring onions (scallions)

lemon

sesame seeds

sun-dried tomatoes

4 Put the sesame seeds on a large plate and very gently press both sides of the fish cakes into them, until the cakes are lightly coated.

5 Pour oil into a frying pan to a depth of about 1 cm/½ in. Heat it gently. Put a small cube of bread in the pan and, if it sizzles, the oil is ready to cook the fish cakes. You will need to cook the fish cakes in several batches.

6 When one side is crisp and brown turn the cakes over carefully with a spatula and a fork, to cook the second side. The fish cakes are quite soft and need gentle treatment or they will break up. Lift them out and put them to drain on kitchen paper. Keep hot until they are all cooked.

COOK'S TIP
Use canned tuna instead of the salmon, if you prefer.

Pepperoni Pasta

Add extra zip to bland and boring pasta dishes with spicy pepperoni sausage.

Serves 4

INGREDIENTS

275 g/10 oz/2½ cups dried pasta
175 g/6 oz pepperoni sausage, sliced
1 small or ½ large red onion, sliced
45 ml/3 tbsp green pesto
150 ml/¼ pint/⅔ cup double (heavy) cream
225 g/8 oz cherry tomatoes, halved
15 g/½ oz fresh chives

cherry tomatoes

green pesto

pasta

double (heavy) cream

red onion

fresh chives

pepperoni sausage

1 Cook the pasta in a large pan of lightly salted, boiling water, following the instructions on the packet.

2 Meanwhile, gently fry the pepperoni sausage slices and the onion together in a frying pan until the onion is soft. The oil from the sausage will mean you won't need extra oil.

3 Mix the pesto sauce and cream together in a small bowl.

4 Add this mixture to the frying pan and stir until the sauce is smooth.

5 Add the cherry tomatoes and snip the chives over the top with scissors. Stir again.

6 Drain the pasta and tip it back into the pan. Pour the sauce over and mix well, making sure all the pasta is coated. Serve immediately.

COOK'S TIP

Use a mixture of red and yellow cherry tomatoes for a really colourful meal. Serve with sesame bread sticks.

Chocolate Cups

Perfect for the chocoholics in the family. Serve with crisp dessert cookies.

Serves 4

INGREDIENTS
200 g/7 oz bar plain (semi-sweet) chocolate
120 ml/4 fl oz/½ cup double (heavy) cream
75 g/3 oz white chocolate

double (heavy) cream

white chocolate   *plain (semi-sweet) chocolate*

1 Break half the plain (semi-sweet) chocolate into pieces and put them in a bowl. Stand the bowl over a pan of hot, but not boiling, water and leave to melt, stirring occasionally. Make sure the water doesn't touch the bowl.

2 Line four ramekins, or similarly sized cups, with a piece of foil. Don't worry about it creasing or scrunching up.

3 Use a clean paintbrush to brush the melted chocolate over the foil in a thick layer. Chill in the fridge until set. Paint a second layer and leave to chill again.

4 Put the cream in a bowl and whisk until stiff. Melt the remaining plain chocolate as before and use a metal spoon to fold it into the cream.

5 Roughly chop the white chocolate and stir it gently into the chocolate and cream mixture.

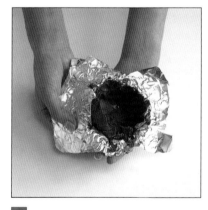

6 Carefully peel the foil off the chocolate cups and fill each one with the chocolate and cream mixture. Chill until set.

COOK'S TIP

Try using white chocolate drops, chocolate-covered raisins or a chopped chocolate bar, instead of the white chocolate.

Ice Cream Bombes

This chilly dessert with warm sauce will have you ready to explode – it's dynamite!

Serves 6

INGREDIENTS

1 litre/1¾ pints/4 cups soft-scoop chocolate ice cream

475 ml/16 fl oz/2 cups soft-scoop vanilla ice cream

50 g/2 oz/⅓ cup plain (semi-sweet) chocolate drops

115 g/4 oz toffees

75 ml/5 tbsp double (heavy) cream

double (heavy) cream

vanilla ice cream

chocolate drops

toffees

chocolate ice cream

1 Share the chocolate ice cream between six small cups. Push it roughly to the base and up the sides, leaving a small cup-shaped dip in the middle. Don't worry if it's not very neat; it will be frozen again before the ice cream melts too much. Return to the freezer and leave for 45 minutes. Take it out again and smooth the ice cream into shape. Return to the freezer.

2 Put the vanilla ice cream in a small bowl and break it up slightly with a spoon. Stir in the chocolate drops and then use this mixture to fill the dip in the chocolate ice cream. Return the cups to the freezer and leave overnight.

3 Put the toffees in a small saucepan and heat gently, stirring all the time. As they melt, add the double cream and keep mixing until all the toffees have melted and the sauce is warm.

4 Dip the cups in hot water and run a knife round the edge of the ice cream. Turn out on to individual plates and pour the toffee sauce over the top. Serve immediately.

Puffy Pears

An eye-catching dessert that is simple to make and delicious to eat, especially when served with whipped cream or natural (plain) yogurt.

Serves 4

INGREDIENTS
225 g/8 oz puff pastry
2 pears, peeled
2 squares plain (semi-sweet) chocolate, roughly chopped
15 ml/1 tbsp lemon juice
1 egg, beaten
15 ml/1 tbsp caster (superfine) sugar

puff pastry

pears

egg

caster (superfine) sugar

lemon juice

plain (semi-sweet) chocolate

1 Roll the pastry into a 25 cm/10 in square on a lightly floured surface. Trim the edges, then cut it into four equal smaller squares.

2 Remove the core from each pear half and pack the gap with the chopped chocolate. Place a pear half, cut-side down, on each piece of pastry and brush them with the lemon juice, to prevent them from going brown.

3 Preheat the oven to 190°C/375°F/ Gas 5. Cut the pastry into a pear shape, by following the lines of the fruit, leaving a 2.5 cm/1 in border. Use the trimmings to make leaves and brush the pastry border with the beaten egg.

4 Arrange the pastry and pears on a baking sheet. Make deep cuts in the pears, taking care not to cut right through the fruit, and sprinkle them with the caster sugar. Cook for 20–25 minutes, until lightly browned. Serve hot or cold.

COOK'S TIP
Try the same thing using eating apples, especially when you have picked the fruit yourself.

Summer Fruit Cheesecake

Making this is much easier than it looks and it tastes so good, it's well worth the effort.

Serves 8–10

INGREDIENTS

175 g/6 oz/¾ cup butter
225 g/8 oz digestive biscuits (graham crackers)
rind and juice of 2 lemons
11 g/scant ½ oz sachet gelatine
225 g/8 oz/1 cup natural (plain) cottage cheese
200 g/7 oz/scant 1 cup cream cheese
400 g/14 oz can condensed milk
450 g/1 lb/4 cups strawberries
115 g/4 oz/1 cup raspberries

milk

butter

lemons

cottage cheese

raspberries

cream cheese

digestive biscuits (graham crackers)

strawberries

gelatine

COOK'S TIP

Always add gelatine to the liquid, never the other way round.

1 Cut a piece of greaseproof (wax) paper to fit the base of a 20 cm/8 in loose-bottomed springform cake tin (pan). Melt the butter in a saucepan over a low heat. Break the biscuits (graham crackers) in pieces, put them in a food processor and whizz until they are crumbs. Stir them into the melted butter until well mixed.

2 Tip the crumbs into the cake tin and use a spoon to spread the mixture in a thin, even layer over the base, pressing down well. Put the tin in the fridge while you make the filling.

3 Put the lemon rind and juice in a small bowl and sprinkle the gelatine over. Stand the bowl in a saucepan of water and heat gently, until the gelatine crystals have all melted. Stir the mixture and leave to cool slightly.

4 Put the cottage cheese in a food processor and whizz for 20 seconds. Add the cream cheese and condensed milk, fix the lid in place again and whizz the mixture. Pour in the dissolved gelatine mixture and whizz once more.

5 Roughly chop half the strawberries and scatter them over the base. Add half the raspberries, saving the rest for decorating the top. Pour the cheese mixture carefully over the fruit and level the top. Return to the fridge and leave overnight to set.

6 Carefully loosen the edges of the cheesecake with a palette knife. Then stand the cake tin on a large mug or can and gently open the clip at the side of the tin. Allow the tin to slide down. Put the cheesecake on a serving plate and decorate it with the reserved fruit.

Carrot Cake

This is full of healthy fibre – yet moist and soft at the same time.

Serves 10–12

INGREDIENTS

225 g/8 oz/2 cups self-raising (rising) flour
10 ml/2 tsp baking powder
150 g/5 oz/1 scant cup soft brown sugar
115 g/4 oz ready-to-eat dried figs, roughly chopped
225 g/8 oz carrots, grated
2 small ripe bananas, mashed
2 eggs
150 ml/¼ pint/⅔ cup sunflower oil
175 g/6 oz/¾ cup cream cheese
175 g/6 oz/1½ cups icing (confectioner's) sugar, sifted
small coloured candies, nuts or grated chocolate, to decorate

sunflower oil

dried figs

cream cheese

self-raising (rising) flour

baking powder

eggs

icing (confectioner's) sugar

carrots

bananas

soft brown sugar

1 Lightly grease an 18 cm/7 in round, loose-based springform cake tin (pan). Cut a piece of baking parchment or greaseproof (wax) paper to fit the base of the tin.

2 Preheat the oven to 180°C/350°F/ Gas 4. Put the flour, baking powder and sugar into a large bowl and mix well. Stir in the figs.

3 Using your hands, squeeze as much liquid out of the grated carrots as you can and add them to the bowl. Mix in the mashed bananas.

4 Beat the eggs and oil together and pour them into the mixture. Beat together with a wooden spoon.

5 Spoon into the prepared tin and level the top. Cook for 1–1¼ hours, until a skewer pushed into the centre of the cake comes out clean. Remove the cake from the tin and leave to cool.

6 Beat the cream cheese and icing (confectioner's) sugar together, to make a thick frosting. Spread it over the top of the cake. Decorate with small coloured candies, nuts or grated chocolate. Cut in small wedges, to serve.

COOK'S TIP

Because this cake contains moist vegetables and fruit, it will not keep longer than a week, but you probably won't find this a problem!

Gingerbread Jungle

Snappy cookies in animal shapes, which can be decorated in your own style.

Makes 14

INGREDIENTS
175 g/6 oz/1½ cups self-raising (rising) flour
2.5 ml/½ tsp bicarbonate of soda
2.5 ml/½ tsp ground cinnamon
10 ml/2 tsp caster (superfine) sugar
50 g/2 oz/¼ cup butter or margarine
45 ml/3 oz/3 tbsp golden (corn) syrup
50 g/2 oz/½ cup icing (confectioner's) sugar
5–10 ml/1–2 tsp water

flour

icing (confectioner's) sugar

golden (corn) syrup

butter

caster (superfine) sugar

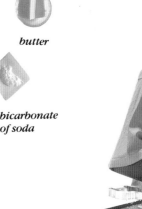

cinnamon

bicarbonate of soda

COOK'S TIP

Any cutters can be used with the same mixture. Obviously the smaller the cutters, the more cookies you will make.

1 Preheat the oven to 190°C/375°F/Gas 5. Put the flour, bicarbonate of soda, cinnamon and sugar in a bowl and mix together. Melt the butter or margarine and syrup in a saucepan. Pour over the dry ingredients.

2 Mix together well and then use your hands to pull the mixture together to make a dough.

3 Turn onto a lightly floured surface and roll out to a 5 mm/¼ in thickness.

4 Use animal cutters to cut shapes from the dough and arrange them on two lightly oiled baking sheets, leaving enough room between them to rise. Press the trimmings back into a ball, roll it out and cut more shapes. Continue to do this until the dough is used up. Cook for 8–12 minutes, until lightly browned.

5 Leave the shapes to cool slightly, before lifting them on to a wire rack, with a palette knife. Sift the icing (confectioner's) sugar into a small bowl and add enough water to make a fairly soft frosting. Put the icing in a piping bag fitted with a small, plain nozzle and pipe decorations on the cookies.

Hot Chocolate & Choc-tipped Cookies

Get those cold hands wrapped round a steaming hot drink, and tuck into choc-tipped cookies.

Serves 2

INGREDIENTS

FOR THE HOT CHOCOLATE

90 ml/6 tbsp drinking chocolate powder, plus a little extra for sprinkling

30 ml/2 tbsp sugar, according to taste

600 ml/1 pint/2½ cups milk

2 large squirts canned whipped cream

FOR THE CHOC-TIPPED COOKIES

115 g/4 oz/½ cup soft margarine

45 ml/3 tbsp icing (confectioner's) sugar, sifted

150 g/5 oz/1¼ cups plain (all-purpose) flour

few drops of vanilla essence

75 g/3 oz plain (semi-sweet) chocolate

milk

sugar

drinking chocolate powder

icing (confectioner's) sugar

plain (semi-sweet) chocolate

soft margarine

vanilla essence

canned whipped cream

flour

1 To make the hot chocolate, put the drinking chocolate powder and the sugar in a saucepan. Add the milk and bring it to the boil, whisking all the time. Divide between two mugs. Add more sugar if needed. Top with a squirt of cream.

2 To make the choc-tipped cookies, put the margarine and icing (confectioner's) sugar in a bowl and beat them together until very soft. Mix in the flour and vanilla essence. Preheat the oven to 180°C/350°F/Gas Mark 4 and lightly grease two baking sheets.

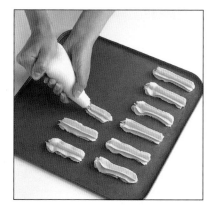

3 Put the mixture in a large piping bag fitted with a large star nozzle and pipe 10–13 cm/4–5 in lines on the baking sheets. Cook for 15–20 minutes, until pale golden brown. Allow to cool slightly before lifting on to a wire rack. Leave the cookies to cool completely.

4 Put the chocolate in a small bowl. Stand in a pan of hot, but not boiling, water and leave to melt. Dip both ends of each cookie in the chocolate, put back on the rack and leave to set.

COOK'S TIP
Make round cookies if you prefer, and dip half of each cookie in melted chocolate.

Strawberry Smoothie & Stars-in-your-Eyes Cookies

A real smoothie that's lip-smackingly special, when served with crunchy stars-in-your-eyes cookies.

Serves 4–6

INGREDIENTS

FOR STARS-IN-YOUR-EYES COOKIES
115 g/4 oz/½ cup butter
175 g/6 oz/1½ cups plain (all-purpose) flour
50 g/2 oz/¼ cup caster (superfine) sugar
30 ml/2 tbsp golden (corn) syrup
30 ml/2 tbsp preserving sugar

FOR THE STRAWBERRY SMOOTHIE
225 g/8 oz/2 cups strawberries
150 ml/¼ pint/⅔ cup natural (plain) yogurt
475 ml/16 fl oz/2 cups ice-cold milk
30 ml/2 tbsp icing (confectioner's) sugar

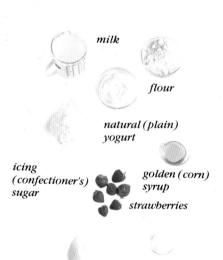

milk

flour

natural (plain) yogurt

icing (confectioner's) sugar

golden (corn) syrup

strawberries

caster (superfine) sugar

preserving sugar

butter

1 First make the stars-in-your-eyes cookies: put the butter, flour and sugar in a bowl and rub in the fat with your fingertips, until the mixture looks like breadcrumbs. Stir in the caster (superfine) sugar and then knead together to make a ball. Chill in the fridge for 30 minutes.

2 Preheat the oven to 180°C/350°F/Gas 4 and lightly grease 2 baking sheets. Roll out the dough on a floured surface to a 5 mm/¼ in thickness and use a 7.5 cm/3 in star-shaped cutter to stamp out the cookies.

3 Arrange the cookies on a baking sheet, leaving enough room for them to rise. Press the trimmings together and keep rolling out and cutting more cookies until all the mixture has been used. Bake for 10–15 minutes, until they are golden brown.

4 Put the syrup in a small, microwave-safe bowl and heat it on HIGH for 12 seconds. Or heat for a minute or two over simmering water. Brush over the cookies while they are still warm. Sprinkle a little preserving sugar on top of each one and leave to cool.

5 To make the strawberry smoothies, reserve a few of the strawberries for decoration and put the rest in a blender with the yogurt. Whizz until fairly smooth.

6 Add the milk and icing (confectioner's) sugar, process again and pour into glasses. Serve each glass decorated with one or two of the reserved strawberries.

TEMPLATES

*These templates are used in some of the projects in the book.
You can either trace them directly from the page,
or enlarge them to the size required following the instructions
at the beginning of the book.*

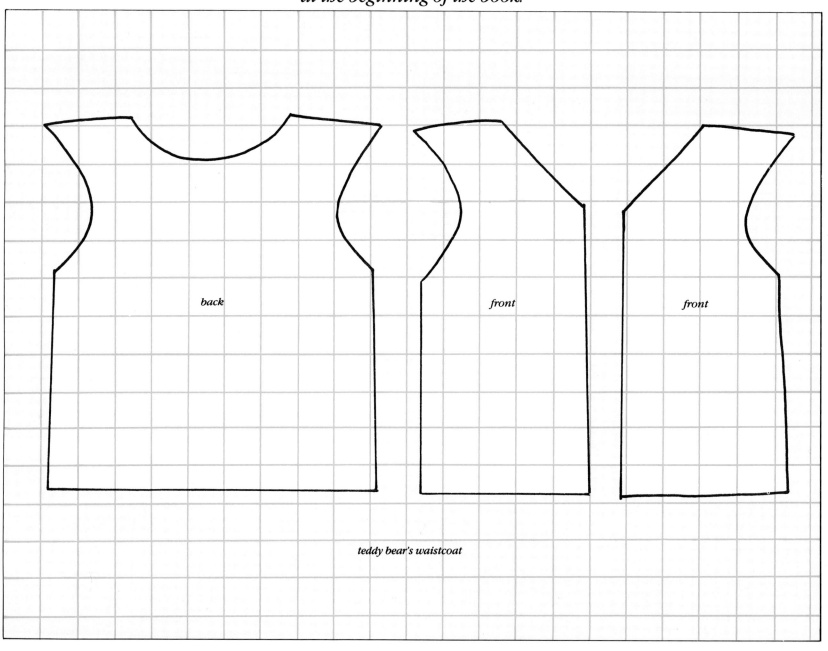

back

front

front

teddy bear's waistcoat

Christmas wreath

dressing-up doll

Christmas wreath

eye mask

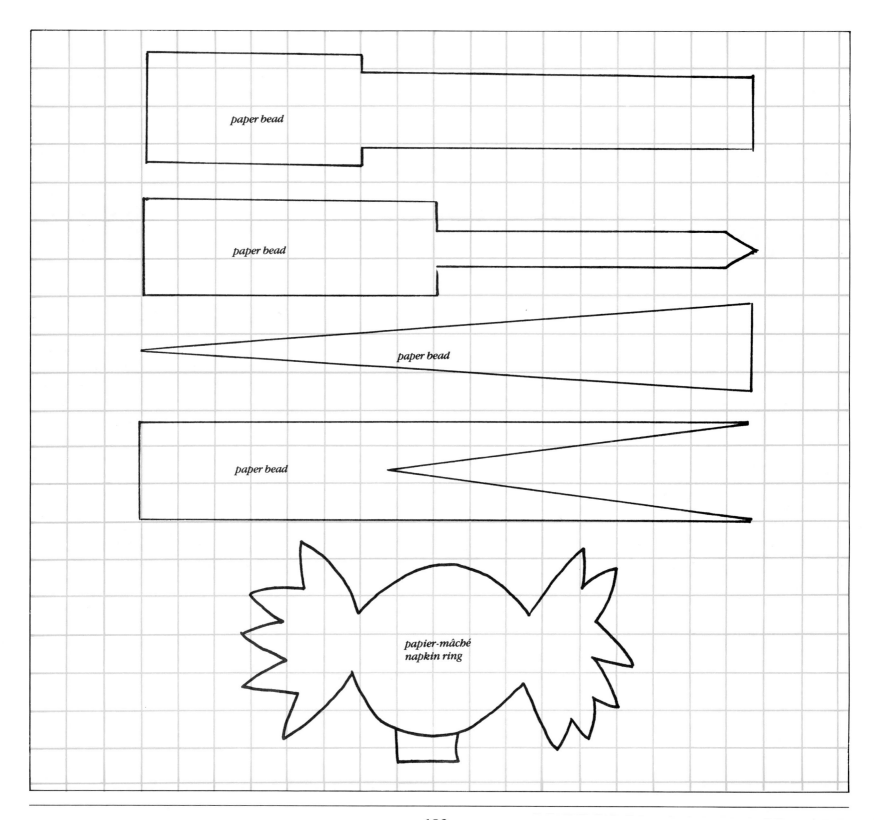

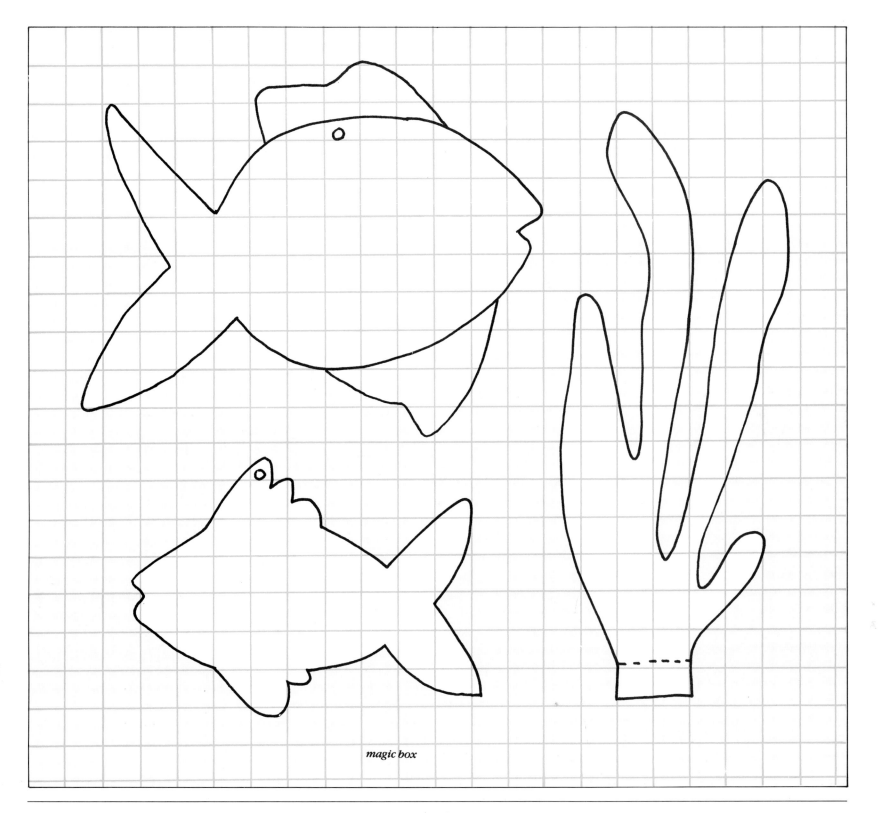

magic box

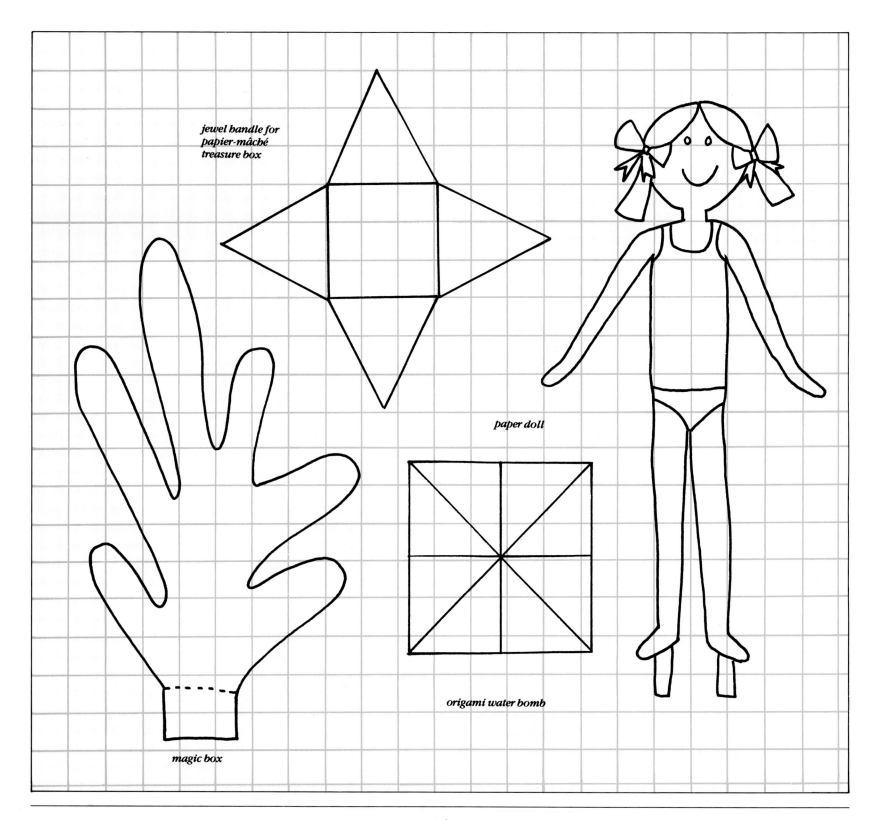

jewel handle for
papier-mâché
treasure box

paper doll

origami water bomb

magic box

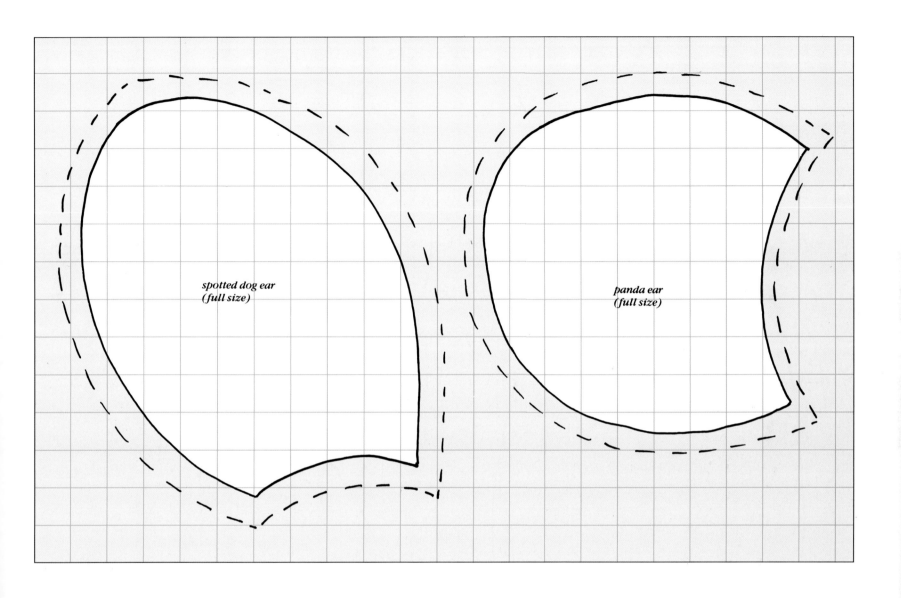

spotted dog ear
(full size)

panda ear
(full size)

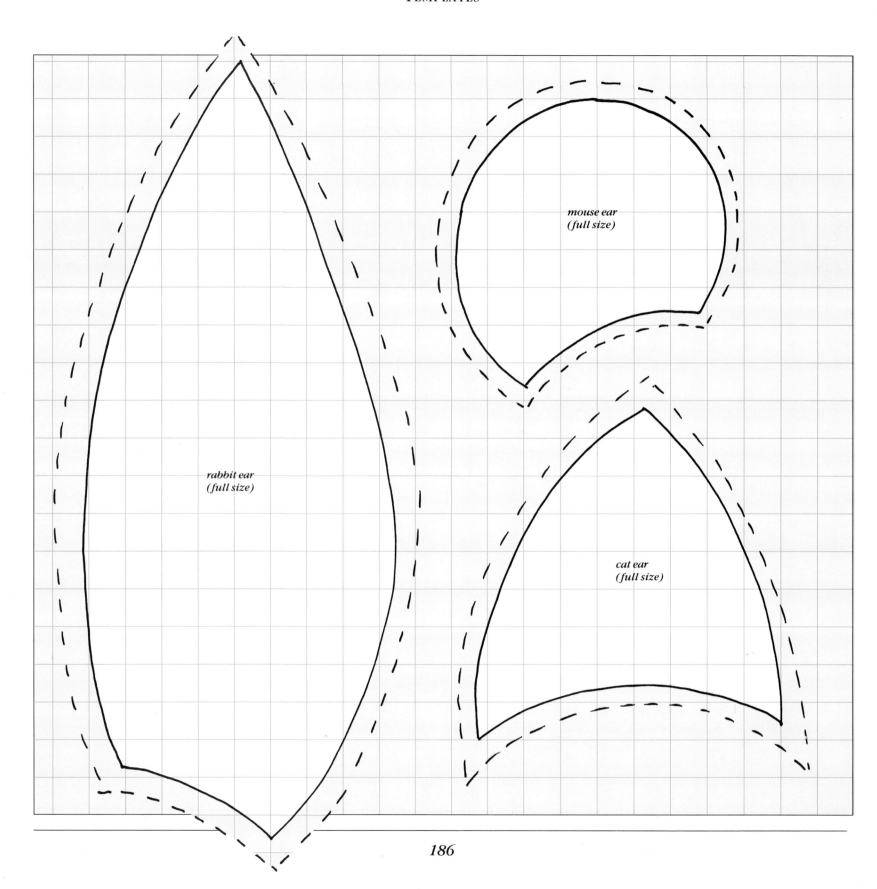

rabbit ear
(full size)

mouse ear
(full size)

cat ear
(full size)

hippy flower
(half size)

cowboy pocket
(half size)

cowboy pocket detail
(half size)

clown button
(half size)

wizard pendant
(half size)

cowboy badge
(half size)

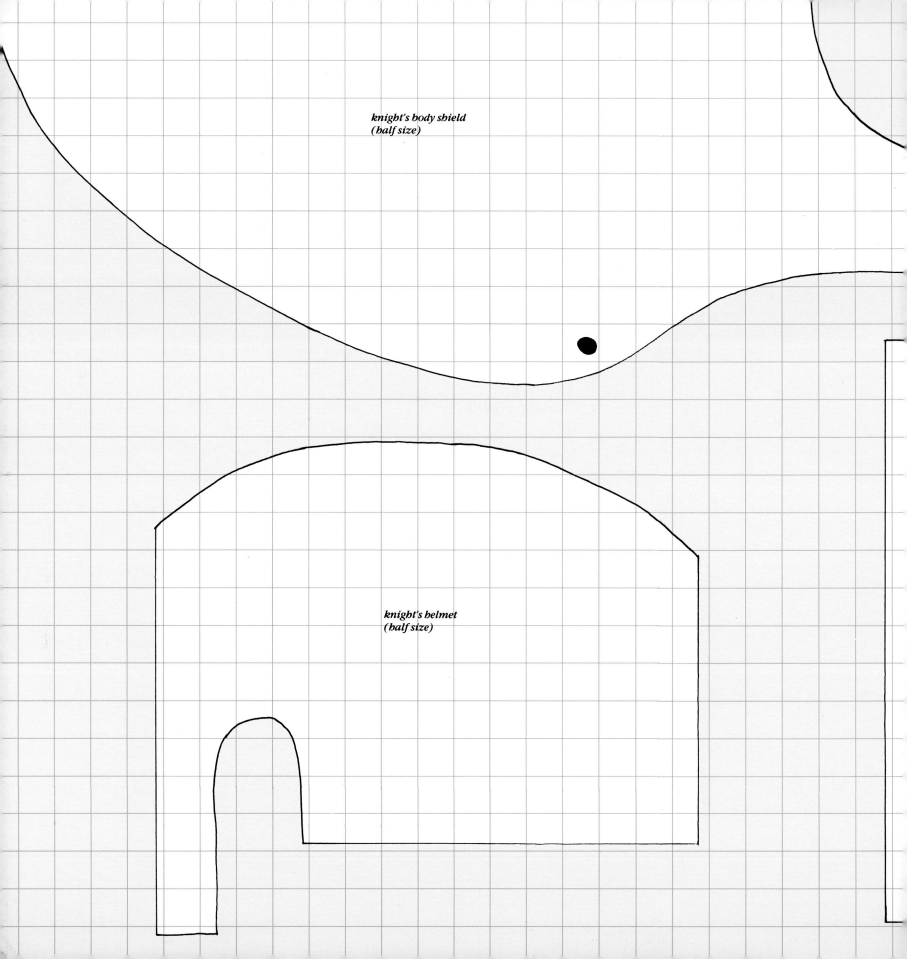

knight's body shield
(half size)

knight's helmet
(half size)

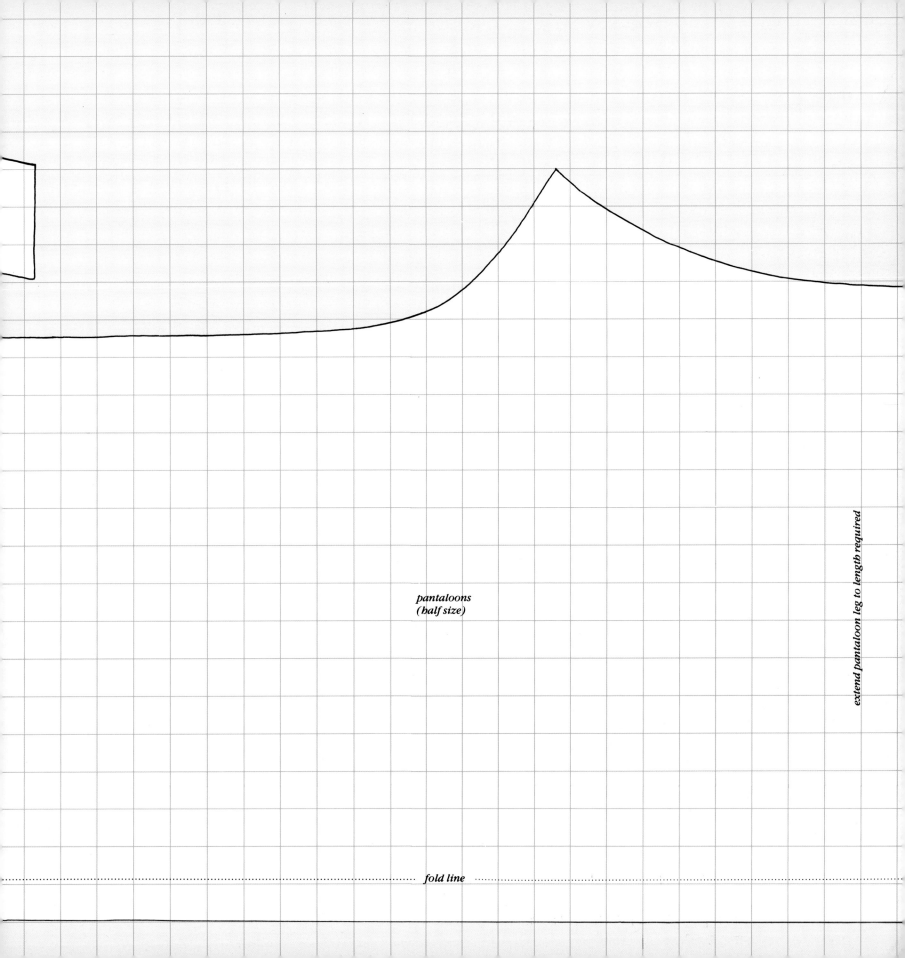

pantaloons
(half size)

extend pantaloon leg to length required

fold line

INDEX